Sexy

The love child of an Au[...] [...]y
Barr was educated at a [...]
in Switzerland. At the age of fourteen she landed her first film
role, in Luigi Fettucine's controversial musical, 'Night of the
Living Zombies'. Although on the threshold of movie stardom,
she sacrificed her film career to devote herself fully to the life
of the jet-set novelist. She now lives in Bel Air, Gstaad and
Monaco with three borzois and a bird of paradise.

Candy Barr claims her heroine and literary mentor to be the
writer Caroline Bridgwood, whose novels *This Wicked
Generation*, *The Dew of Heaven* and *Magnolia Gardens* are also
published by Pan Books.

Candy Barr

Sexy

Pan Original
Pan Books   London, Sydney and Auckland

All characters in this book are fictitious, and any resemblance
to actual persons, living or dead, is purely coincidental.

First published 1988 by Pan Books Ltd,
Cavaye Place, London SW10 9PG
9 8 7 6 5 4 3 2 1
© Caroline Bridgwood 1988
ISBN 0 330 30568 9
Phototypeset by Input Typesetting Ltd, London
Printed and bound in Great Britain by Richard Clay, Bungay, Suffolk

To my brother
Richard (Chub)

One

'I'm so hungry I could eat a scabby donkey!'

Jay Cathcart, self-styled media whizz kid and guru of High Tack squatted down on bare floorboards and propped himself against the wall. 'Chuck us the phone, will you, and I'll have some food sent over . . . hey, that would be quite a cool name, actually, "The Scabby Donkey"—'

'JAY! For God's sake, you haven't told me yet what you think of it!'

' . . . Hmmm, Japanese or Thai, or . . . Sorry – think of what?'

'Of this! Of this place!'

Jay and his brother's girlfriend, Heidi Plunkett, were in an empty loft conversion on top of a block of shops and offices that overlooked the Fulham Road. Heidi was dressed in a very grubby white raincoat, with a clipboard in one hand and a cellnet phone in the other. Jay was wearing Gaultier and a pink PVC knapsack.

'Hey, no probs, I think this place is great. Just right, really.' Jay surveyed the whitewashed walls and the network of pipes and cables that striped the ceiling. 'It's the location I'm worried about really. I mean, it's not exactly the West End, is it?'

'Ah, but that could be to our advantage,' said Heidi quickly, flicking through the notes on her clipboard.

'According to my research, of the twenty-five to thirty-five year olds buying property in London, sixty-eight per cent of them bought in Fulham. And what is their chief point of access with Central London? . . .'

'The Fulham Road.'

'Got it in one. It even runs in a straight line, so the stupidest of debauchees couldn't get lost on their way here . . .'

'Right, you've got my vote. I'll buy it. The question is, will you front it for me?'

Heidi looked down at her dirty coat, and her ageing loafers, worn down to wafer thinness on the soles.

'I don't know, Jay. I don't exactly look like a night club hostess, do I?'

'Oh don't worry,' Jay waved one hand airily as he phoned the takeaway with the other. 'I'll get one of our stylists to take care of that.'

Heidi could picture the results: she would be turned out like a poppy television presenter, with a cute little quiff of peroxided hair and magenta lips. She grimaced.

Jay strode over to the intercom and admitted the delivery boy with his brown paper carrier of California Sushi rolls. 'Hey, look, Heidi, I mean, what's the problem? You're the one who went out and found this place for me. I thought it was because you wanted in. I thought you agreed that we were going to become joint owners of our own night club.'

Heidi bit her sushi roll too hard, catapulting vinegar rice down the front of her raincoat. 'I did. I mean I do. But I suppose I'm naturally more cautious than you, and I'm concerned about what we're getting into—'

'A licence to party, that's what. Wall-to-wall bodies and a coke dispenser in every toilet . . .'

Heidi scowled at Jay. 'I mean the money. I've done the research Jay, and it takes hundreds of thousands to get a decent club going. And it can be as much as ten years before you start turning in a profit. I don't know whether I want the commitment, and the grinding insecurity—'

'Forget it, babe, there isn't going to be any insecurity!' Jay waved his arms expansively and showered a frosting of vinegar rice onto Heidi's short, spiky hair. 'I'll just pump in the profits from my other business interests.'

'You mean the video company?' Heidi asked doubtfully. Jay's latest seven inch promo had been nothing short of disastrous – shot in black and white it starred an all girl band and used BBC Light Entertainment has-beens as extras (including several ex-*Blankety Blank* guests), in vaudeville costumes from *The Good Old Days*.

Jay had a visionary gleam in his eye, a sure indication of the tastelessness of his new project. 'Forget the videos, man! That's just lining the pockets of all the other schmucks in the business, by encouraging the punter to go out and buy someone else's products. No, I'm going to out-shmuck all the others by getting in at the front of the queue. I'm going to start recording the discs themselves. So what do you say?'

'Okay,' said Heidi warily. 'I'll give it a whirl. At the decision-making level. But I don't know about actually running the place.'

'I don't see why not,' said Jay. 'After all, it's not as though you've got a job at the moment, is it?'

He was referring to Heidi's recent departure from the tabloid *Daily Meteor*, where she had once been a star feature writer. But when the editor had asked her to go and root around in a rock star's dustbin, to glean evidence of his rumoured split with his wife, she had resigned, on the grounds that her career could only plummet further into the gutter if she agreed.

'I'll think about it,' she said in the end. 'Can we get together tonight and talk about it?'

3

Jay shook his head. 'Sorry, got a date. With Saskia.'

'*Saskia?*' Heidi was stunned. 'But you had a date with her last week.' In all the years she had known Jay, he had never – not once – been seen with same girl twice. A stream of pretty, air-brained girls had been used and discarded faster than kleenex in a flu epidemic.

'I know,' admitted Jay, staring at his hand tooled loafers with a sigh.

'Jay! Are you feeling okay? Is it serious?'

'It could be.'

Heidi put her hand on his brow. 'Would you like an aspirin?'

Jay gave another martyred sigh. 'It gets us all in the end.' He grabbed the phone and got to his feet. 'We'll talk later. Until then . . . well, here's to the Hottest Disco in Town! Partners?' He held out his hand.

Heidi hesitated. 'Only if you're sure about the money? . . .'

Jay pointed to his suntanned, blandly handsome face. 'Look here, babe, what do you see?'

'A piece of rice stuck to your lip?' suggested Heidi.

'What you see,' went on Jay, 'Is a Svengali. Think Brian Epstein. Think Quincy Jones. Think Stock, Aitken and Waterman.'

'You mean you've discovered a rock star?'

'I have discovered an act . . .' Jay tossed his mobile phone in the air and caught it deftly with the same hand, before tucking it away in his waistband. ' . . . that's going to make the Beatles look like one-hit wonders!'

Sammi-Dawn Thwort was having a bad day.

Not only had she broken her longest fingernail on the

toaster, but she had also left her favourite lip pencil on the back seat of a taxi.

She discovered this loss as she arrived for a photo shoot at a West End studio. On the pavement outside there was the usual small huddle of autograph hunters. Sammi-Dawn usually accepted this situation as the lot of Britain's best-known topless model; part and parcel of her life since she had won the *Daily Meteor's* Chick of the Year Competition. But because of losing the pencil she was in a vicious mood, and didn't draw the usual 'smiley' underneath the scrawled 'luv Sammi'.

'I'll have to go all the way back to bleedin' France if I wanna nother one like it,' she lamented to the make-up artist. 'I bought it in San Trop.'

Once her lips had been outlined with an inferior product, and slicked with cyclamen gloss, and her heavily high-lighted blonde hair scrunched and tousled, Sammi undressed for the session: on this occasion the All Colour Sammi-Dawn Christmas Calendar. Wearing nothing but a pair of silky French knickers and five-inch heels, she teet-ered across the studio to the set, which was draped in pink fun-fur. Her 38DD cup trembled as she walked, causing the photographer's assistants to turn their heads tactfully away. It was well known that Sammi-Dawn didn't like people staring at her boobs.

Dave, the photographer, had vast experience of topless work, and had developed a line of gentle chat to put the model at ease.

' . . . That's lovely sweedart . . . just relax . . . if you could just stick that bit of miseltoe between your teeth . . . got a pet, have you, Sammi, got a little dog?'

'No,' said Sammi.'

'How about a little cat, then?'

'No.'

'A budgie?' asked Dave hopefully.

'No. Hate birds.'

'So you haven't got any pets at all at home?'

'My dad's got six Rottweilers,' Sammi grimaced. 'Hate dogs.'

Dave accepted that his softening up routine was never going to work on the irredeemably monosyllabic Sammi.

'Okay,' he said wearily. 'Stick your tits out for me please . . . that's lovely, but you're still scowling . . . think of the fee, darlin', think of the . . . *that's* it, lovely! . . . hold it there . . . keep 'em towards me . . .'

Sammi was back in the dressing room changing into a leopard skin loincloth for the jungle scene when her manager arrived.

Gerry Gyles had managed some of the greatest rock stars of the seventies, and had been close friends ('I mean, we were *this* close') with all of them until they had discovered how much of their earnings went into his mock-Queen Anne mansion in Sunningdale. He still liked to drop in a Bryan or a Rod or an Elton when the conversation became a bit drab. He wore a gold ear-ring in one lobe, and baggy linen suits with the sleeves permanently scrunched up above the elbow.

No-one was surprised at his arrival, least of all Sammi-Dawn, who usually ignored him anyway. Gerry trailed behind his most important client like a vigilant nanny, seemingly bursting with protective pride at her success. He carried a phone with him everywhere and talked on it constantly, giving the impression that time spent looking after his clients was a generous sacrifice on his part. He even employed a chauffeur so that he could sit in the back of the car with the telephone and talk his way through traffic jams.

'Can you wrap this one up quickly, love?' he asked Sammi-Dawn, punching a number into the phone as he talked. 'You and me have got a very important appointment later this morning. And I *mean* important. We are talking mega-quids here, mega-stardom, the full monty.'

Sammi scowled at him in the mirror as she touched up her violet mascara. But Gerry knew the territory and was unperturbed. 'What's your greatest ambition, love?'

This was something of a rhetorical question, since the entire register of topless models in Britain shared only two ambitions between them: a) to be a rock star b) to be a film star.

'I wanna be a rock star.'

'Exactly. And what has your uncle Gerry done for you? He's only given you a chance to have your dreams come true? So chop, chop love, let's get this one over with!'

Sammi positively cantered back to the set and posed her way rapidly through March, April and May, before being whisked off in the back of Gerry's customised Mercedes.

'So where are we going?' she demanded.

'Just a minute love, I'm making a call,' said Gerry, who was on the line to the local laundry about his dry-cleaning bill. He made a lot of important-sounding noises about contracts and finance before hanging up. He dialled his auntie's number in Blackburn.

Sammi opened her mouth again but he waved his hand. 'One second, love, I'm on a long distance . . .'

The car finally pulled up in Maida Vale, outside a very ordinary looking five-storey terrace.

'What's this then?' demanded Sammi.

'Look up there.'

Two workmen were up ladders, fixing discreet chrome letters above the front door. Sammi spelled them out one by one, sticking her tongue out and screwing up her eyes with the effort.

'R-A-P-I-E-R . . . "Raper?", what's that?'

'It's the new Rapier Recording studio. They're just starting it up, Ivo Cathcart and his lot. And I know you

7

know who Ivo Cathcart is, because you've had your piccie taken with him haven't you?'

Sammi scowled. 'He's dead ugly,' she said. She was reluctant to admit to Gerry that she had actually had an affair with Britain's most notorious entrepreneur. She knew he would try and force them back together again for publicity purposes and she didn't want that.

'Ugly or not, he's the key to your future. Him and his brother, who's going to be running this outfit. So smile, love, okay?'

With her face positively splitting in two, Sammi was marched up the steps and into the half-finished foyer. They were met by a Beastie Boy look-alike with his peaked cap on back to front.

'This is Tim Goldsmith, Sammi-Dawn, Rapier's A&R man.'

'Aynar?'

'Never mind about that, love. He's the man who finds them new recording artists.'

Tim Goldsmith was hopping from foot to foot with nervous impatience. Jay Cathcart had told him he must sign Sammi at any cost, and he was anxious to get it over with before she could change her mind. If she had one.

'Er . . . first things first, eh? The contract . . . Would you like to come this way?'

Sammi was dragged into an office, where a Badoit water was thrust into one hand and a biro into the other. She signed, without reading, a contract which handed eighty per cent of her revenues over to Rapier Recording Incorporated and stipulated in the small print that in event of a dispute between herself and Rapier, she forfeited all recourse to law. There were at least ten other penalty clauses allowing Rapier to dump her without a penny, but even if she had bothered to read them, she wouldn't have cared. She was going to be a star. Gerry had read them, and he didn't care.

'Right. Super. Next – the publicity photos.' Tim glanced at Gerry, who was picking his teeth with a letter-opener. 'Are you going to tell her, or shall I?'

Gerry hastily grabbed his phone and started jabbing in a number with an air of great preoccupation. 'The thing is, love . . . the record company want you to change your image a teensy weensy little bit . . . just for promotional purposes, you understand.'

'What's wrong with my image?' Sammi asked suspiciously.

Tim looked at her fluffy pink mohair sweater, her white leather mini skirt and the dyed Canadian lynx jacket.

'Nothing . . . er, of course it's very nice, but if you're going to be a rock star, you're going to have to look a little more, er . . .'

'Raunchy?' suggested Gerry over the mouthpiece of his handset.

Before she could protest, Sammi was whisked into a small cubicle, where three stylists were sucking their teeth in anticipation. The door was locked behind them and the sound effects began: the loud whirring of hair-dryers, the rattle of chains and the ripping of denim. And howls of protest from Sammi.

She emerged half an hour later, teetering on a pair of black spike-heeled ankle boots with chains dangling off them. Her stone-washed jeans had strategically placed tears underneath her naked buttocks and her breasts jutted from a studded leather basque. Her hair had been teased and back combed into a top-knot which trailed its blonde tendrils over sooty, heavily-kohled eyes and a white-painted pout.

'Sensational!' enthused Tim.

'Fantastic!' agreed Gerry. 'What d'you think, love?'

'Can't breathe,' complained Sammi.

'Don't worry about that,' said Tim. 'We won't be much longer now. Just one more little thing. Last – and least important. The voice test.'

'If I can't breathe, I can't sing' said Sammi, who couldn't sing anyway.

'Just give it a little go,' said Tim, dragging her into the studio and sticking her in front of a naked mike with a copy of 'Somewhere Over the Rainbow'.

'Okay, when you're ready . . .'

Sammi opened her mouth, fractionally, and began what amounted to little more than a hum. It was almost in tune, but barely audible. Gerry looked concerned.

'Don't worry, that was just a test. Now let's see what we can do with it.' He motioned to the engineers to plug in the synths and the computerised voice box.

The result was astonishing. Still hardly moving her lips, Sammi was emitting an echoing, high-pitched growl, a cross between Eartha Kitt and Jimmy Somerville.

'Perfect,' shouted Tim from the gallery. 'A new recording star is born!'

Down below, Sammi-Dawn let out a loud wail of discontent, 'Aw, no!' she yelled, without the aid of synthesisers. 'I've broken me best nail in these soddin' zips!'

A few miles south, in Kennington, Leofred Plunkett was having a good day.

He had bought a new suit. It cost him six hundred pounds in Savile Row, and was consequently the most expensive item not only in his wardrobe, but in his entire flat. Its cut was exquisite, Italianate, its cloth superfine wool, as light as a feather. Leofred had to take two valium before he dared wear it.

It's an investment, he told himself, as he sprang cheerily up the steps of Drummond Industries, where he worked. Six weeks ago he had been made a vice president of the company by its chairman, Sandra Snell.

'A touch of nepotism, but who gives a toss?' had been the verdict of Sandra. She and Leofred had become close friends the previous year when they were respectively a member of the typing pool and a humble graduate trainee. Together they had exposed an insider dealing scandal and taken over the company board at one stroke. 'It's got a nice ring to it, too, hasn't it? Vice president. President of Vice. I like it. Only you'll have to try and be a bit more vicious, Leof.'

Blowing six hundred quid on a suit was as vicious as he had managed so far. But he would work on it. He started by curtly ignoring Alf, the doorman, as he wished him 'Good morning.' Mesmerised by the transformation, Alf stared after him with his mouth open.

Leofred took the lift up to his office. Since last year's coup, he had moved from the broom cupboard he occupied as a graduate trainee to more agreeable surroundings. The room wasn't large – Drummond wasn't that sort of company – but at least he could move a piece of paper without knocking the contents of his desk to the floor, and didn't have to sit with his feet in the waste paper bin.

'Vicious,' he said aloud. 'Think vicious.' He screwed up a draft report that had just landed on his desk and tossed it out of the window into the street below. He was beginning to enjoy himself.

Leofred's next stop was the Typing Pool. Here he was usually treated with a teasing familiarity; the faintly conde-scending indulgence that women reserve for men who represent no threat.

'Cor!' shouted Debbie, wolf-whistling at Leofred's suit.

'Look at you, eh? Where d'you get that bit of shmatta, then?'

Leofred blushed, by pre-conditioned response.

''S one of Terry Wogan's cast-offs, I reckon,' giggled Debbie.

Leofred spun round suddenly on his heel and faced them. 'Have you got that report I sent down?' he snapped.

Silence.

'Well, I'd like it on my desk by the end of the morning please.'

The Girls stared after him without speaking, wondering what had come over the normally mild-mannered and diffident Leofred.

On his desk, Leofred found a message from the Chairman, requesting his presence in her office. He sauntered in there, hands in pockets.

'Well, what d'you think?'

'You look a right pratt,' said Sandra, replacing the brush in her bottle of nail varnish. 'Your shirt's buttoned all wrong.'

Leofred looked down, and it was true. He sighed. It seemed that hard-hitting business dynamos were born and not made, and he wasn't one of them.

'Sit yourself down, darlin',' said Sandra. 'You and I have got to have a little chat. Coffee?'

Leofred nodded. Sandra flicked the intercom button with a polished talon. 'Coffee for two, please, Jules,' she instructed her male secretary.

Leofred took in her appearance. She had acquired a certain polish since her rapid promotion from the typing pool. The highlights in her hair now cost a hundred pounds a time and her silk blouses were by famous designers. Power suited her; she looked well. In fact today she was positively blooming. But beneath the surface Sandra had changed little. She was still the brazen, foul-mouthed tart-with-a-heart she'd always been. She still had beefcake plastered all over the walls, even if it was now tasteful nudes in glossy frames rather than the pages ripped from Playgirl that she started with.

Julian, Sandra's secretary, came in with the coffee. He was an effeminate, slim-hipped youth with Latin looks and expensive taste in clothes. So expensive, that more than once Leofred had found himself wondering how they were purchased on a secretary's salary.

Julian was making a big fuss of Sandra, spreading out a napkin on her lap to protect her suit, brushing her thigh as he did so. And Leofred couldn't help noticing that Sandra blushed like a schoolgirl when he touched her, placing a hand on his wrist and murmuring 'Thank you, Julesy' in a register quite unlike her usual shriek.

When they were alone, Sandra returned to normal. She looked Leofred straight in the eye and said 'I'm leaving, sunshine.'

'*What?*'

'Since you and me are such good mates I wanted to tell you before anyone else.'

Leofred was breathless with surprise. 'But Sandra . . . why?'

She looked down at her fingernails. 'Well, I've had a good run for me money in the last year, had a few laughs, but this power thing's not all it's cracked up to be . . . but there is another reason . . .' She paused. 'I'm in the club.'

'I'm sorry? Which club?' Leofred pictured a sort of female freemasons.

'The pudding club, dickhead! Up the spout! Knocked up! . . . I'm having a baby, you idiot!'

'Oh, I see.' Leofred thought it would be rude to seem too shocked. 'I didn't realise you were . . . I mean, I didn't know there was anyone . . .'

'If you're wondering who the father is,' said Sandra

13

baldly. 'It's Julian. Usually the boss knocks his secretary up, I know, but this time it's the other way round.'

'Oh,' said Leofred. 'Ah, I'd always assumed he was . . .'

'Gay,' said Sandra. 'No he's not. Q.E.D.'

'But aren't you—'

'Too old? Forty-one's knocking on a bit, I'll grant you, but it's not unheard of.'

'Well . . . I hope you're, er—'

'Happy? I'm over the bleedin' moon. It's been so long since the other two, I'd forgotten what it was like. I've never felt better. And Julian's thrilled.'

'So you're going to be a working mum?' Leofred almost pleaded, not wanting Sandra to leave.

'No way, sunshine! I want to enjoy it while I can. Which brings me on to your future. You know I can't nominate you as my successor don't you? They'd only say twenty-three was too young. Even though you have got the suit for the job.'

'I wouldn't want to much, anyway,' confessed Leofred.

'That only leaves two choices. We can promote someone from within – and you know as well as I do that the only candidates are a load of boring, middle-aged deadbeats – or the board can get a head-hunter to bring in someone from outside. I chose the outsider option, and I've just been told who he's going to be.'

Sandra tossed a file marked 'PERSONNEL – CONFIDENTIAL' across the desk to Leofred. He glanced at the photo, then read the *CV*. The new man was called Michael Broome and he had a double first from Oxford, and an MBA from Harvard. And a rowing blue. Somehow it was the blue that made Leofred feel more depressed than anything else.

He went back to his office feeling completely dispirited. Then he noticed that the shock of Sandra's announcement had made him splash some coffee onto his lap, staining his new suit. And he wondered how a day that had started so well could go so badly wrong.

Ivo Cathcart was sitting at his desk at Rapier's newly finished head office, staring at a small bottle of pills and feeling very excited.

This massive glass-plated building in London's Tottenham Court Road was the hub of his empire; an empire that was built on supermarkets and cinemas, film companies and Japanese factories. And – since his successful takeover the year before, the Star pharmaceutical chain. And now their research and development people had come up with one single product that could be so successful he would be able to sell off all his other interests.

He picked it up and looked at it. A plain brown bottle, such as a pharmacist would dispense, containing large, ovoid pink pills. The label on the bottle said simply 'ZXT 45'.

Ivo pocketed the bottle and set off to the third floor where he was about to address a meeting of his marketing managers. All his marketing managers. They had been summoned from the corners of Europe. As Ivo walked into the room, their eyes were on him, expectant. They knew this would be something big.

He gave them a brief smile, then clicked his fingers at his assistant who was waiting at the back of the room. Instantly the lights were dimmed and the screen on the wall illuminated. A slide clicked up into view. It was blank but for one word, in enormous capitals, at its centre.

SEXY.

The lights went up again. Ivo was still smiling at them. 'Well,' he said to the assembled throng of pinstripes, 'are you feeling sexy?'

There was no response save an astonished silence.

'Okay,' said Ivo, unperturbed, 'take a look at this video.'

A short piece of video film was projected onto the screen. It was a commercial for a well-known brand of condoms. A young man came to the point of asking the lady shop-assistant for them, but chickened out several times before he could bring himself to mention the offending item.

Ivo interrupted the video at this point and put the lights on again. He stood in front of his marketing team, who were agog by now, as if he was going to make a speech. But instead he put his hand in his pocket and whipped out an unfurled condom. He waved it in their faces and it made a damp, flapping noise. 'Not very sexy, is it?' he asked.

There were a few muffled snorts from the younger members of his audience.

'What about the ladies amongst you?' went on Ivo, letting his eye alight on the seriously well-coiffed women executives. 'Does the sight of this – or the thought even – turn you on?'

Ivo was well into his stride now, demonstrating the qualities that had earned him overwhelming business success. His ugliness was mesmerising, the movements of his stocky, muscular body full of power.

'What about this?' he asked, and like a conjuror pulled a diaphragm from his pocket, followed by a tube of spermicidal jelly. 'Looks a bit like a wok, doesn't it? You could cook your dinner in there.' He smeared the jelly all over the diaphragm and squeezed its edges. It catapulted across the room with great force and landed on the projector.

'The point I'm making, if you haven't already seen it,' said Ivo, wiping his jellied fingers on his handkerchief, 'is that the very things that are supposed to make it all right for us to have sex, i.e. contraceptives, are a bloody turn off.'

One or two of the more hip marketing men nodded in agreement.

'The Pill has lost popularity in the last five years but no-one's come up with a decent alternative. And since AIDS has been a fact of life, that means there's still a massive market waiting to be exploited . . . so, what if someone came up with a product that was effective against conception, sexually transmitted diseases *and* was fun to use as well?'

Ivo paused just long enough to make sure he had everyone's rapt attention, before reaching in his pocket again, this time for the bottle of pills.

'Well, here is such a product, ladies and gentlemen. Known at the moment as ZXT 45.' He took out a pill and held it up for their inspection. 'Stunning in its simplicity, and yet even more stunning in its application; what we have here is the marketing opportunity of the decade. Later on I'll be handing around copies of a full lab. report, but let me just try and summarise its use. This tablet is used by the woman and simply . . . er . . .' He blushed slightly as his eyes locked with one of his lady managers ' . . . er, inserted. Internally. Its chemical properties are such that it is a powerful spermicide, a de-activator of the AIDS virus *and* it has something of an aphrodisiac effect on the user. Let's just say . . .' he interjected a winning smile, ' . . . it starts up an itch that just has to be scratched.'

More silence, then a burst of spontaneous applause.

'Thank you. And now I'd like to hand over to Tony Hendry for his thoughts on the marketing potential of ZXT 45 – Tony . . .'

Tony Hendry, Rapier's marketing supremo and a man with thirty years experience, was almost lost for words. He cleared this throat as he stood up, thinking of the consequences if this pill was handed round at his wife's coffee mornings in Godalming, which was what often happened to new products he worked on.

'Er . . . clearly this should be aimed at the yuppie market,' he pronounced, falling back on a familiar old cliché, 'but we'll need to do some very detailed market research first. I propose that Paul Latchkey here—' he indicated his right hand man, a keen young graduate from Keele University, '—should get in touch with the largest market research agencies and invite them to submit proposals for an extensive survey. With the results we should know exactly how to position the product, and therefore how to market it.'

There were a few suppressed yawns – this was what Tony Hendry said about every product he encountered.

'In the meantime, our own team will be collating all available information. Tell me Ivo, what is the history of the product's use so far? Have there been any field trials?'

'Not exactly,' said Ivo, with a glint in his eye. 'But I'm working on it.'

On his way back from work that night, Ivo stretched out in the back seat of his white Bentley Continental and asked the driver to put some Wagner on the in-car stereo. The dramatic, overblown strains of Wagner exactly suited his mood of triumph. A standing ovation at the meeting and a product that would set the world alight, well, justifying the massive investment he planned.

Everything was going his way. At thirty-nine, his career was reaching a pinnacle. And he and Heidi were at last managing to co-exist in harmony, without the continual fights that dogged the early stages of their affair. She was mellowing, he reflected, growing up . . .

The car pulled up outside their house. Or rather, their

houses. Heidi still insisted on token independence, but in practice they spent much of their free time together, so Ivo had solved the problem by buying two houses in a Knightsbridge mews, right next door to one another. So Heidi still had the symbolic front door of her own, to which Ivo had no key. There was one connecting door between the two houses but it was kept locked except in cases of bad weather or emergency.

He could hear the thump of Heidi's stereo from the mews. As a gesture, he rang the doorbell.

'Come on in!' Heidi shouted as she opened the front door.

Ivo followed her retreating back into the sitting room.

'Darling . . . remember I said I'd take you out for dinner tonight? . . .'

The bottle of pills rattled in his pocket.

' . . . well how about trying something new?'

Two

Waking up the next morning was a shock for Heidi Plunkett.

There were strange tingling sensations in her legs and abdomen, and dull cramps all over her nether regions. She had a hangover, but it was not in the usual place.

She was alone in the king size bed. It was five to nine and Ivo was long since gone. She propped herself up on the pillows and screwed up her face with the effort of collecting her thoughts. What had happened the night before? Had she got drunk?

Then she remembered.

Ivo and his bloody pills.

With a monumental effort, Heidi attempted to reconstruct the events of the past twelve hours. Ivo had been abnormally hyperactive, positively excited, when he returned from work. They had had a swift drink and then he'd dragged her protesting up to the bedroom. He'd dimmed the lights, switched on the soft music. He'd started kissing her, as usual, then edged his way down the bed, his tongue everywhere . . .

Then suddenly: 'What the hell's *that* Ivo?'

'Just a little . . . er . . . um . . . sex aid.'

'Just a minute.' She'd struggled. 'I haven't got my thing in.'

'No need to worry about that, darling, I'll take care of it . . . just lie back and relax . . .'

She'd felt something hard and small and cold, then a fizzing sensation.

'How d'you feel?' Ivo had been anxious to know.

'Great . . . sort of relaxed and yet strong . . . sort of . . . MNNFGRH!!

At this point she had found herself leaping on top of Ivo and engaging him in combat for a very long time.

In Heidi's opinion the power of the pills was so extraordinary it was worth putting up with this hangover. Her brain felt like cold mashed potato . . . hadn't something happened afterwards as well, seemingly hours and hours later? Oh yes . . . OH GOD!

Heidi sat bolt upright in bed, remembering.

Afterwards they had lain in one another's arms and she had felt wonderful, different, somehow more relaxed and more tranquil than she had ever felt before. And the conversation had run thus:

IVO: *Have you found yourself another job yet, darling?*
HEIDI: *No, not yet.*
IVO: (nuzzle, nuzzle) *Only I've been thinking . . . now you're out of work, perhaps this is the time for us to really settle down, get married . . . I mean, you haven't got a job and you must do something . . .*

And what had she said? She'd been so zonked out she just lay there and went 'Mmmmm.' Good God! A housewife! The end of the bloody world!

Heidi leapt out of bed like a singed cat and fell on the phone, thumping in Jay's number.

'Jay, Jay . . . about what we discussed—'

'Huh?'

'Running the club on a day to day level. I'll do it! . . .'

*

At that precise moment, Leofred Plunkett was thundering down the Bakerloo Line towards Lambeth North.

He was adopting his usual position, i.e. comatose, shoulders slumped forward, eyelids lulled closed by the soporific swaying of the carriage.

Then he saw the newspaper of the passenger opposite. It was The *Financial Times*, and on the back page was a photograph which looked provocatively familiar. Where had he seen that face before? He opened his eyes further.

'NEW BROOME SWEEPS CLEAN' said the headline.

Leofred leaned across and tapped on the paper. 'Er . . . excuse me, do you think I could take a quick look at your paper? It's just that—'

'Sure,' said the girl who was reading it.

He folded the paper carefully in half and examined the small print of the article.

It has just been announced that the new chairman of Drummond Industries will be Mr Michael Broome, 46.

When questioned yesterday, Mr Broome made no secret of the fact that he was planning to instigate a bloodless coup. He said. 'Their management style has become something of a laughing stock in the industrial world, and I fully intend that this will change.' Mr Broome refused to comment further on his plans, but confirmed that the changes would affect staff of all levels, and added 'Heads will roll.'

Leofred buried his head in the newspaper and groaned.

At the new Rapier Recording studios, Sammi-Dawn Thwort, pop megastar, was arriving for her first recording session.

Gerry Gyles had planned the day like a military campaign. First, Sammi was mobbed by a large crowd. Her regular fans were there, of course, but their numbers had been boosted by kids from the local Barnardo's home, who were bribed with free doughnuts and ten pence pieces to spend on the fruit machines.

Then several out-of-work photographers had been hired to stand in the foyer and fire off a lot of flashguns as they captured Sammi's new image for the gossip columns. She was wearing wrap-around shades, even though it was a wet, cloudy, August day, a different pair of jeans with a different set of rips, fingerless lace gloves and a lace camisole that was straining at the seams.

'Great stuff', commented Jay Cathcart, who was on a flying visit to oversee his new investment. 'It's all looking very good. Great. Right. I'll leave you in the capable hands of young Tim. Time I wasn't here . . . Bye y'all.'

Jay disappeared in a flash of Armani, and Sammi was dragged off into the press office to give an interview to reporters from *Time Out* and '*Q*' magazine.

'Now, about your new single, Sammi, can you tell us something about it?'

'Don't know nothink about it. Haven't made it yet.'

'*You know what it's like though, love!*' hissed Gerry. '*I played the demo to you in the car, remember?*'

'Could you perhaps tell us what it's called?'

Sammi looked blank. She couldn't remember if they'd omitted to tell her or if they'd told her but she just couldn't remember. All she knew was that this was a lot harder than topless modelling.

'That's obviously confidential at the moment,' said Gerry hastily, 'But I'll tell you boys something . . .' He tapped the side of his nose in a man-of-the-world sort of fashion.

' . . . it's going to be perrritty raunchy!'

'How about your private life, then, Sammi? Going out with anyone?'

Sammi opened her mouth.

'Sammi dates a lot of guys,' Gerry interjected quickly. 'But there isn't one special man in her life at the moment.'

'What about Barry?' whined the object in question.

'Barry?' the journalists salivated eagerly.

'Her brother . . .' said Gerry. 'She's getting confused . . . my client's under a lot of pressure . . . showbiz . . . music business . . .'

Sammi was marched quickly along the corridor towards the studio. 'Listen, you're not to see that moron, d'you understand?' Gerry was referring to the faithful Barry, Sammi-Dawn's part-time sidekick for the past seven years. 'I don't want the press seeing you with an unknown motor-bike messenger. It won't look good. You understand?'

Once in the studio, they were introduced to writer/producer Vince Morell, who had been flown in speci-ally from Philadelphia to record Sammi's single. Vince, who hailed originally from Barnstable, wore shirts with pictures of ladies' heads on them, unbuttoned to the waist to reveal his medallions. They in turn rested on his beer gut. Sammi stared, mesmerised, at this round furry dome.

''Kay, I've written this song specially for you little lady,' said Vince, who had written it five years earlier. It's called 'I'm Feeling Sexy'.

'Great!' enthused Tim Goldsmith, who was hovering at the side of the great man.

'I'll run through it for you.' Vince started to growl in a voice like sandpaper on gravel. ' "*Touch my body; gimmee a thrill/I'm a wild beast and I'm ready to kill/Cos I'm feeling sexy, sexy as hell . . .* " Then there's the chorus, you see.'

Vince waited for signs of approval.

'Great!' said Tim.

'Great!' said Gerry.

Sammi said nothing.

''Kay, are we ready to go, people?'

Sammi was pushed into a tiny booth with massive headphones clamped on her head. An anonymous disco backing track was switched on and the engineers primed their tapes ready for recording.

But it was hopeless. Sammi-Dawn couldn't memorise the words, and when she was given a score, she couldn't read them off fast enough to keep pace with the backing track. They tried again and again, but the only obvious tangible result was that Sammi became more and more sullen.

"Kay, okay . . .' said Vince, waving his hands for them to stop. He rubbed his sweaty brow and then wiped the sweat on his belly. 'We'll dub in somebody else's voice for the verses. All you have to do is sing the chorus. Do you think you can manage that, little lady?'

With Gerry mouthing the words at her, Sammi managed to memorise the chorus, but the result still wasn't good enough. She sang it in a feeble, half-hearted way with as much expression as a goldfish.

'How the hell are we going to get her to open her mouth?' sighed Vince, towelling down his stomach.

Sensing the premature end of his client's career, Gerry stepped in. He climbed into the booth and lifted off Sammi's headphones.

'Sammi, love, you know Maria Meloni?'

Maria was Sammi's chief rival in the topless pin-up world, a voluptuous nineteen year old of Italian extraction.

Sammi's eyes narrowed.

'Well, I want you to imagine that she's arrived at String-fellows and she's not only wearing the same dress as you, but she looks a lot better in it. Then she accidentally on purpose sticks her stiletto in your toe as she walks past you . . . to dance with *your* boyfriend. How do you feel?'

Two blobs of puce started to spread over Sammi's cheeks.

'Good girl! Now, I want you to think of that when you're singing.'

The backing track was cranked up again. Eyes still

narrowed, Sammi opened her mouth and bawled with uncontrolled rage.

"*Cos I'm feeling sexy . . . sexy . . . SEXY!*"

'Thank Christ!' said Vince. 'Make sure you print it!'

'Heidi, this is Saskia. Sas., this is Heidi.'

Heidi shook hands with Jay's new light of love, employing her fiercest stare of appraisal. In return she was rewarded with a beaming smile. Saskia Barron was not only stunningly pretty, with long honey blond hair and a complexion like warm marble, but she was sweet too. In the true sense of the word. She might have failed finger-painting in kindergarten but she was kind to animals.

After the introduction, Heidi resigned herself to feeling permanently depressed by the contrast between the two of them. With her rain-spiked hair and her grubby mackintosh she felt like a cross between Hilda Ogden and Roland Rat.

Jay had told her to meet him at the Fulham Road loft immediately after he had signed the lease papers on the place.

'We'd better get to work on the place now,' he told Heidi, 'because we're going to hold the official opening in a week.'

'A *week!* Jay, we'll never do it!'

'Yes we will, won't we Sas? Sas. is going to lend us a hand.' He gave Saskia a beaming smile and hugged her closer to him. The two of them seemed to be joined together by some invisible glue, and it was making Heidi feel uneasy.

'Very well,' She averted her eyes in the direction of her clipboard. 'I made some notes on the way here. Number one: a name.'

'No probs. I've already sussed it. I read somewhere in

the deeds about the site once being the estate of a guy called Richard de Coverley. So I thought we'd name it after him.'

'What – "*Richard's*"?'

'No, "*Dick's*".'

Heidi gave a heavy sigh but made no comment. It was probably very appropriate to the clientele.

'Okay, number two – decor.'

'Bagsy I'm in charge of that!' said Jay. 'I know exactly what to do with it to make it totally groovy and crucial. And Sas.'ll help me. She's done an interior decorating course, haven't you, Sas?'

She also does a passable impression of a ventriloquist's dummy . . .

'Three – recruitment.'

'I thought you'd be best at that, Heidi.'

'Okay, so who will we need? . . .'

'I've already found us a barman. My mate Andy from school. He's cool. But we will need a hat-check girl, waitresses, a bouncer—'

'Wait a minute, Jay! I can't interview bouncers. I don't know anything about bouncing.'

'Well now's your chance to find out. I've already phoned the employment agency and they've promised to send over a few candidates. They should be arriving . . .'

Jay checked his Piaget, which he had adopted in favour of the Rolex ('Too many people wearing them now')

' . . . just about now.'

Right on cue, the doorbell buzzed.

'Ah . . . I was wondering if you could give me a job.'

'*Leofred!*' said Jay and Heidi in unison.

'What the hell are you doing?' Heidi asked her younger brother. 'You should be at work.'

'I've just been sacked,' said Leofred. 'I thought you might have something for me here . . .'

'Bouncer?' said Heidi hopefully.

'No, no, no . . .' Jay unglued himself from Saskia and put a heavy hand on Leofred's shoulder. 'He'd be wasted. I've got something much better in mind. Why don't you come into the office and discuss it? . . .'

The bouncing candidates started to arrive. Questions about ambitions and hobbies seemed rather irrelevant, so Heidi devised a practical intitiative test.

'Okay then,' she said to the first applicant, a diminutive but pugnacious Glaswegian. 'I want you to imagine that I'm a Hell's Angel, and I'm not very good at taking no for an answer. How would you handle the sit—'

She suddenly found herself several inches off the ground, suspended by the scruff of the neck.

'See yooo, Jummy..see thess? . . .'

The hard crown of his skull made contact with her stomach.

'I see . . . Well . . .' Heidi waited for her feet to return to the ground. 'We'll be in touch . . .'

The Glaswegian was followed by an ex-wrestler with body odour so bad that he was sure to deter *bona fide* patrons, and a mild-mannered Sikh who failed the practical by being too polite. By the time the fourth applicant arrived, Heidi was in the mood for doing some bouncing herself. Biting back a bestial snarl, she flung the door open so it rocked on its hinges.

And found herself face to face with a six foot four Adonis, complete with suntan and smile wrinkles around the eyes. Heidi gripped the doorhandle, consumptive with lust.

'Hi!' said the demi-god. 'My name's Liz.'

At the headquarters of Rapier Industries, there was a furious clocking up of overtime in the marketing department. Keen young Paul Latchkey was closeted away with a fascinating work entitled '*Contraceptives and the General Public – a definitive guide to consumer attitudes.*'

There was doubt about it, no two ways of looking at it, not even for a marketing man. Paul did not like what he read. Consumer resistance to change in the field of contraception was very high. Dangerously high. The public didn't like to experiment. It was as simple as that. Paul closed his eyes and all he could see was a huge cloud looming over the future of ZXT 45.

The door opened, with no warning knock. Paul opened his eyes and there was the Great Man himself. Ivo Cathcart. Always a bit of a teacher's pet, Paul blushed fetchingly.

'So, how's it going?' Ivo rubbed his hands eagerly. 'Is it looking good?'

'Er . . . yes. Yes it is.'

Paul kept his fingers crossed until Ivo had gone out of the room. In fact it was looking bad. It was looking just about as bad as it possibly could. And the expensive survey was only going to confirm this fact. And he – Paul Latchkey – would be the one who had to convey this to Ivo Cathcart.

He sat at his desk for a very long time wondering what on earth he was going to do about it.

Jay/Saskia and Leofred faced each other over the makeshift desk in the back office of *Dick's*.

'So, what do you think then?' asked Jay in an avuncular fashion.

'Singing telegrams?' Leofred said doubtfully.

'The demand's enormous. And you'd have everything you needed, right here under this roof. You could share this office. You could put up your advertising up here. And you'd have a supply of punters. When people are out clubbing they get pissed enough to book anything. So, whaddya say?'

'Well . . .'

'I'd let you keep sixty per cent of the profits. No, seventy. In fact we could run any number of businesses out of this place. Sas. was thinking of running a dog-walking business, weren't you, Sas?'

'Where will I get my . . . singers from?'

'Well you could start with the fall-out from Heidi's recruitment drive – look.'

In the main club-room, Heidi was drilling the potential waitresses, getting them to weave between two tables holding a very small tray packed with brimful glasses. Standing at her side, laughing very loudly, was a barrel-chested young man with a tan that left Jay's in the pale.

Jay hated competition. As soon as an opportune moment presented itself, he beckoned Heidi over.

'Who the hell's that?'

'Isn't he wonderful?' Heidi gave a deeply uncharacteristic giggle. 'He's called Lez with a 'z' and he's Australian. He's our new bouncer.'

'How're you going, mate?' asked Lez. wringing Jay by the hand until his eyes watered visibly. 'This your sheila? Wow, not bad, eh?'

Saskia coloured prettily (how else?). Jay opened his mouth to make a threat then considered Lez's pectorals and thought better of it. He addressed Heidi.

'How are you getting on with the waitressing staff? . . . oh my God, what the hell is that?'

He pointed to a very plump woman of indeterminate age, who was making a surprisingly good job of weaving between the tables. 'Heidi, come on, we can't have people looking like that! What will it do for the club's image?'

Heidi was forced to agree. 'But what am I going to tell

her?' she asked desperately. 'I mean, it's obvious that she's a much better waitress than most of them. I can't just say we don't want her because she looks awful!'

'Why not?' asked Jay. 'She does.'

Heidi treated him to an outraged feminist glare. Leofred intercepted it.

'Er . . . I've got an idea.' Since that morning his sympathy for job-seekers had risen one hundred fold. 'I could give her a job in my end of the business.'

'What as?' asked Jay. 'An uglo-gram or a fatto-gram?'

But Leofred had already asked her to step into the office with him.

'What's your name . . . Mrs . . . er?'

'Joan. Joan Grimmins. And it's Miss, not that that's anything to do with you.'

Leofred put this rudeness down to an extreme sensitivity about her looks. Joan really was a sorry sight. Her hair was lank and uncut, her round, smooth face devoid of any make-up. She probably wasn't much older than thirty, but the shapeless frumpiness of her clothes contributed to the impression of middle age. And she was fat. It looked as though there were several cushions stuffed down the waist-band of her trousers.

Leofred was so fixated with this image that he began to waffle.

' . . . too good for the waitressing side . . . party entertainment business . . . good money . . .'

'You want me to be one of those fat ladies who take off their clothes in other people's houses.'

'No, no, no!' said Leofred. 'Goodness no! People just want to see a jolly, smiling face. And you sing a funny little song—'

'Oh all right then,' said Joan sourly, as though it were she who was doing Leofred a favour. 'I'll take it. But only if I can personally vet the jobs I get sent on. Is that understood?'

'Yes,' said Leofred weakly. 'Anything you say.'

Sammi-Dawn and Gerry finally left the studios in Maida Vale at eight o'clock.

Both of them were exhausted. Gerry's raspberry linen suit looked as though he'd slept in it for a week in a dirty station waiting room, and Sammi had huge panda rings of mascara around her eyes.

They stumbled into the back of Gerry's Mercedes and slumped against the white leatherette seats. He swigged from a hip flask of Scotch and lit two cigarettes in rapid succession.

'Right – where's it to be tonight, then? The Hippodrome? The Limelight? . . .'

'Plumstead,' said Sammi. 'I wanna go home to me mum'n'dad in Plumstead.'

This was serious. Sammi rarely acknowledged the existence of her parents, let alone showed any filial feeling.

'But Sammi, love . . . you're a rock star.'

'Don't wanna be a rock star.' Sammi's lip trembled. 'And me bleedin' legs are cold.' She pointed to the generous rips in the thigh of her jeans.

'Come on, babe, it's not that bad! I'm going to get you personal appearances, game shows, charity nights. You're going to be a Very Big Celebrity.'

Sammi sniffed. Once she would have given her eye-teeth, yea, the entire contents of her make-up bag, just to be photographed with a celebrity. Now she was one herself, she didn't like it. Even she could see the irony in that.

*

At nine o'clock, Heidi Plunkett stood on a corner of the Fulham Road, looking for a taxi.

She hugged her clip-board to her chest, exhausted. During the course of the day a whole staff had been hired, decorators and designers commissioned, glasses ordered, ashtrays, loo rolls . . .

Suddenly, out of the gloom, an enormous animal sprang from nowhere and almost knocked her down. An enormous Australian animal.

'Hoi!' said Lez. 'What a welcome sight! A beaut. woman standing on a street corner. Waiting for me, weren't you? So we could go out and get ligless.'

'Really, no, I . . .'

Heidi was confused. If Lez thought she was beaut in her present, bedraggled state, he was either blind, or besotted, or insane.

'Listen, there's a really great pub just down the road there – we can be there in two shakes of a wallaby's dick.' Lez pointed out the genial hostelry, a hundred yards or so in the Fulham direction.

'Really, honestly, I couldn't even walk that far.'

'No need to. I'll carry ya.'

Heidi found herself swept up in a pair of strong arms, as if she was a bag of laundry. (She even *looked* like a bag of laundry). It felt rather nice, but it was her duty to protest, however feebly, as she was deposited on a vinyl banquette in full view of the regulars of the Goat and Braces.

'A poncey green drink with flowers in it for you . . . and a few tubes for me.'

Lez had six cans of lager, which he arranged in a row in front of him.

'I'd rather have one of those than this washing up liquid.'

'Women should't drink beer,' said Lez. 'It makes them fart.'

'Er . . . where did you get your sun-tan, Lez?' Heidi choked back her green drink. 'It's done nothing but rain here all summer.'

'Israel, mate, on a kibbutz. Working as a volunteer. And I volunteered, believe me.' Lez's leathery face creased up in a wink.

'Oh, I do, I do . . . what was it like? Out there, I mean.'

'Beaut. Just beaut. Great weather. Everyone living the simple life. Working hard, partying hard. Plenty of laughs. And people were free, if you know what I mean.'

Heidi did, only too well. She'd always longed to visit Israel herself. ' . . . And London?'

'It's okay, you know, now I've got a job?' Lez's sentences all ended on a rising syllable, as though he was asking a question. 'But I find the people a bit . . . you know.' He pursed his lips.

'Affected?'

'Yeah, that's right. And they're so obsessed with things, material things. All the time it's *my* Porsche, *my* dinky little townhouse, *my* CD player . . .'

Heidi pushed her Organofax and her remote telephone bleeper down into her handbag, well out of sight.

'Tell you what, though. How about us going back to your place and counting the tiles on your bedroom ceiling?'

Heidi made the noises of refusal, trying desperately to push the image of Lez's naked brown torso from her mind.

'Why not? You married, or something like that?'

'Something like that.'

Leofred was hailing a cab to take him to the tube station when he saw Joan Grimmins lumbering along on the other side of the street. Once again, despite his exhaustion, he felt sorry for her.

'Can I give you a lift?' he shouted as he climbed into the cab.

She nodded, and Leofred asked the driver to do a U-turn and pick her up. 'I'm only going as far as South Ken. station,' he explained to Joan, who sat in ungrateful silence. 'But you can catch a tube from there.'

'That's no good to me,' said Joan, as if Leofred had set out to inconvenience her. 'I can't use the underground. I'm allergic.'

'Oh, I'm sorry. Perhaps the driver would take you on. Where do you live?'

'Cricklewood.'

'Nah, guv, can't do Cricklewood. Going off duty.'

'Tell him to drop us at your place,' said Joan. 'And you can order me a mini-cab.'

Swallowing a retort, Leofred suffered the long, trundling journey to Royal Oak, where he'd bought a tiny flat on a huge mortgage.

'You'll have to pay,' Joan told him without a hint of apology. 'I haven't got any change.'

Leofred fumbled with his keys, in a hurry to get rid of the grim Miss Grimmins.

'How about a drink?' she asked.

'Er . . . no thanks, I think we'd better get in and—'

'No, I meant how about you giving me one.'

Leofred searched the fridge, but he had no beer or wine. Eventually he found a bottle of cognac with a dribble in the bottom. 'Here's some brandy, but there won't be very much each, I'm afraid.'

'Never mind.' Joan snatched the bottle, poured the contents into one glass and drank it in a gulp. Leofred stared, disbelieving. First he'd been sacked, then he'd worked in a madhouse all day, now this. His need for a stiff drink had been unsurpassed.

He stumbled to the telephone, but as if they had some

telepathic sense of foreboding, none of the local mini-cab drivers were willing to go to Cricklewood.

'Perhaps you could walk? . . .'

'Of course I couldn't! I'll spend the night with you.'

'Er . . . ah . . . Joan, I don't—'

'You don't think I want to sleep with you, do you? Good God, what do you take me for?'

More relieved than insulted, Leofred rushed off to get spare blankets. 'I'll make you up a bed on the sofa. You'll be very comfortable.'

'No I won't!' retorted Joan. She pulled back the sitting room curtain and pointed below to the railway track and sidings that served traffic between Paddington and the West country. The 10.52 to Swansea roared past, right on cue. 'It's far too noisy. I'll have your bed. You can have the sofa.'

'Er . . . right.' For some reason Leofred found himself staring, mesmerised, at her cushion shaped belly.

He complied with Joan's wishes without protest. You have to feel sorry for her, he told himself as he tossed and turned on the narrow Chesterfield. Probably no-one's ever been nice to her, so she's never had any example . . .

He fell into a shallow, troubled sleep and dreamed of being suffocated by pink rubber cushions.

Three

Heidi Plunkett was turning into a telephone.

Or so she felt, as she prepared for the opening night of *Dick's* night club.

Sitting at her desk in the back office, she scarcely had to replace one of the two receivers in its cradle before it buzzed again. She had the two phones permanently appended around her face, like a bizarre pair of earrings. When she stood up and left her desk, she was haunted by the shrill whining of her aircall bleeper. And from a string round her neck hung two small black call retrievers, one for her home answering machine and one for the club.

Three phones rang. One was Leofred's, on the tiny desk that he had in the corner of the same office. He answered it with a barely-enthusiastic 'Plunkett's Strippograms' and Heidi picked up the other two, asking one to hold and propping it on her left shoulder.

'*Dick's* publicity office. How can I help you? . . .'

It was yet another enquiry from the press about the opening. They wanted to know in advance what the decor was like, who would be there etc., so that they could write up the piece for their editor without having to drag themselves away from the bar of El Vino's in Fleet Street.

'The decor will resemble the interior of a Parisian brasserie in the 1920s', droned Heidi in her best impression of a parrot, 'There will be globe lights, dark wood, colour-washed walls and stained glass panelling. The club will be staffed by waiters in traditional long aprons . . .'

In fact this was all lies; a complete fairy story. Jay had ordered that no-one was to know the real truth about the interior of the club until they set foot in it on the first night. In this way the hacks who didn't bother to turn up would be revealed as the lazy spongers they were, and those who attended would be stunned into writing a flattering piece. Heidi thought it was rather a shame that the club would be nothing like a Parisian brasserie, but Jay had brushed aside her fit of whimsy.

'What we are aiming for,' he told her, 'is massive hipness.'

The journalist also wanted to know who was on the guest list.

'There will be celebrities from many different professions . . . politicians, actors, top models, a certain under-age chat show host . . . and the opening ceremony will be performed by . . .' Heidi gritted her teeth. She had been instructed not to lie about this fact. ' . . . by Rapier Records new star, Sammi-Dawn Thwort, who's going to be singing her new hit single.'

As far as Heidi was concerned there were at least two lies in the last statement – 'singing' and 'hit'. She hung up and turned her attention to the caller on hold. As she repeated the last conversation, verbatim, over the line, she allowed her eyes to fix on the open door and take in what was happening in the club.

Alf, the handyman, was helping the two designers to cover their handiwork with what looked like enormous silk dust-sheets, so that the aesthetic thrill of pleasure could be saved until an appointed moment. Until then the guests would be stumbling around in semi-darkness.

Alf had been the doorman at Drummond Industries, and

had been sacked in the great coup. As a key member of Sandra Snell's petticoat cabinet, Leofred had felt a shared guilt, and had asked Heidi if she could find a job for a diminutive septuagenarian. He wanted to go on being a doorman, and had even brought his old uniform in a Safeway carrier bag. But Heidi had only been able to offer him odd jobs. The position at the door was, after all, already occupied by Lez.

She watched Lez now, lifting crates of mixers. He worked in a slow deliberate way, looking at a crate from all angles before embracing it, as if trying to guess its weight. He was stripped to the waist, and a thin film of sweat coated his naked brown torso. Every so often he would take a Dick Whittington handkerchief from his back pocket and wipe himself down.

This time he spotted Heidi watching him and turned the process into an animal display, rubbing the handkerchief very deliberately over his pectorals.

'G'day' he said.

Heidi waved, which was sufficient provocation for Lez to stroll into the office. He positioned himself on the corner of her desk like some dangerous big cat. His thigh muscle bulged ominously onto her press releases.

'Um . . . Lez . . .'

'You're looking very tasty in that blouse,' he commented, looking straight down her cleavage.

Why did he keep saying these things to her, Heidi wondered, when she was clearly looking no more than averagely all right? Would he say them regardless of who it was sitting behind this desk, or could he in some way sense . . . Of course she was attracted to him. And yet he was different from Ivo in every way possible.

'Lez . . . haven't you got an awful lot of crates to shift?'

'Shifted the buggers.'

'I see . . . well, the thing is, I'm really awfully busy.'

Right on cue, one of her phones rang.

'Righto, I'll shove off then,' said Lez good-naturedly, heaving his thigh off her desk. 'No worries.'

Heidi steeled herself to go through the publicity soliloquy.

'Heidi. Ivo.'

'Oh . . .'

'Listen, I was just checking that I'm going to see you at the club opening tonight—'

'Well of course you will. It's my job!'

'Just wanted to be sure you be there, that's all.'

'I'll be here. No worrie— . . . I mean, no problem.'

Heidi frowned at the telephone. Ivo was acting very oddly. And he wasn't the only one, either. Jay had been whizzing around the club with a very strange look on his face all morning. There was no sign of Saskia either, which was also strange.

'Jay!' Heidi attempted to flag him down as he passed the door. 'Jay, can I have a quick word with you about—'

'Sorry, babe, no time. Big night tonight, and all that . . .' He paused long enough to annoy Heidi with a wink. ' . . . in more ways than one . . .'

In an uninspiring corner of greater London, Bexley Heath to be precise, there were even stranger goings on.

A field worker from Good Results Research Limited was standing on the doorstep of a house in Rosamond Avenue. He checked his clipboard and saw that he was to make random calls on the side of the street with odd numbers 1–23. He rang the doorbell of number five.

'Er, Mrs, er . . .' asked the nervous researcher, an unprepossessing, long-backed lad called Neil.

'Fosdyke. Not that that's any of your business.'

Neil was dealing with an archetypal harridan, wearing a flowered apron and looking like Michael Palin in drag. 'What d'you want, anyway? I'm not giving any money to charity, if that's what you're after. Especially if it's run by pop stars.'

'Er, Mrs Fosdyke, I'd like to ask your opinion on a new product we're researching . . . you see—'

'Well what is it then?'

'It's er . . . um . . .' Neil couldn't quite bring himself to utter the word 'contraceptive'. He was going to have to scrap the results of this particular interview anyway. The client was only interested in the views of women aged between eighteen and forty-five, and Mrs Fosdyke was obviously over the limit. To walk away as soon as the door was opened was against company policy, so a shortened version of the interview had to be carried out before the search for more suitable candidates could resume.

Neil took out a sample of ZXT 45 and handed it to Mrs Fosdyke.

'What's this for then, arthritis? It better not be one of those American drugs that's responsible for killing thousands of innocent pensioners! Because if it is, my lad, I'm calling the police, I can tell you! My neighbour, Mrs Snow, her mother—'

'ZXT–45–is-the-latest-development-in-anti-conception techniques,' babbled Neil, quoting from the product description, 'It-is-simply-inserted-in-the-vag—'

'Filthy creature! You'd better be off before I do call the police! That's typical of attitudes today, that is. I blame it on the schooling. If we hadn't have had comprehensives, no doubt we wouldn't have had AIDS either . . .'

The hapless Neil ran down the path and fell on the doorchimes of number eleven. His relief at finding a woman under thirty-five was quickly overshadowed by the fact that she was in her negligée. She asked him if he would come upstairs and demonstrate his new product.

' . . . well, that's what I always say to those boys who sell tea-towels and dusters,' said Mrs Elvey of number eleven, widening her eyes in mock-innocence. 'And if you're not prepared to demonstrate, then I'm not prepared to answer a lot of silly questions about it . . .'

The lady of the house at number fifteen was seventy-five and deaf, and thought he was a boy-scout doing bob-a-job. Number nineteen was only too glad to answer the questionnaire, but had a PhD in Chemistry and sidetracked him with questions he couldn't answer. Number twenty-one answered 'don't know' to everything, and number twenty-three hit him over the head with a squeegee as soon as he said the word 'insert'.

Neil was seriously considering putting in a claim for danger money. He limped off to the phone box at the end of Rosamond Avenue, to telephone Paul Latchkey at Rapier and let him know that things were not going very well.

Paul Latchkey was already aware that things were not going very well.

When he put down the phone after reassuring Neil, he checked his notepad. In only two days he had received ten such calls from Good Results field personnel. This was an unprecedented situation – usually they would pass on any difficulties to their own managers when they returned to the office. Clearly this product was a tough one to get results on.

But that was only a very small part of the problem. What was really worrying Paul was that the interviews successfully completed were not what Rapier had hoped for. There was a mounting pile of completed questionnaires on his desk, and they made very disappointing reading. Eighty per cent of those in the targeted age group, for example, said that they were spending less money than ever before on contraceptives. Only thirty per cent thought there was room for an alternative contraceptive on the market.

Paul picked up a questionnaire and flicked to the section which invited the consumer's comments. *'Wouldn't trust something as small as that to stop a baby'* read one. *'Not with my hubby, anyway.'*

'WHAT'S AN AFRO-DIZIACK?' demanded another. *'SOMETHING TO DO WITH DARKIES?'*

He sighed. He was not particularly concerned with the ignorance of housewives in Bexley Heath, Barrow-in-Furness and Leamington Spa, but he *was* concerned about his own future at Rapier Industries. He had his eye on Tony Hendry's job, but he wasn't going to get it without a few successful marketing campaigns up his sleeve. Being allowed to supervise this most important project of all was an enormous break, but it wasn't going to get him anywhere if . . .

If it all fell through at the market research stage. He imagined going and presenting these results to Ivo Cathcart. Ivo would be forced to call off the whole venture. And he, Paul Latchkey, would ever after be associated with Ivo's first, and only, entrepreneurial slip-up. The stigma would rub off. If, on the other hand, he told Ivo what he wanted to hear . . . bolstered his ego . . . fired him with enthusiasm . . . he, Paul Latchkey would be covered with glory. And what if the product did fall flat on its face? By the time that happened, he would already have been promoted and there would be a dozen other departments involved who could help absorb the blame . . .

Paul picked up the first computer assessment of the statistics and examined it, sucking his pen. What if that '80%'

there were simply turned into a '30%'? And supposing that '30' were changed into an '80'? . . .

RING-RING . . . RING-RING . . .
    'Hullo – Plunkett Strippograms. How can I help you?'
    'It's me, you daft bum-wipe! Sandra.'
    'Oh, Sandra.'
    'So, how's it going then, the life of the independent businessman?'
    'Okay, you know . . . fine really.'
    Leofred wasn't prepared to admit to anyone, not even Sandra that he wasn't enjoying it. The problems were not financial, as he might have supposed when he first started out. So far he had even turned in a modest profit. Since the first day of recruitment he had taken on several other 'performers', had advertised on a small scale in the local press, and a steady trickle of engagements was coming in. His own job should really have been quite simple. All he had to do was take telephone bookings and allocate them to a member of his staff who best suited the description of what was required. For example, Graham was very good at penguin-o-grams, and Sally, a ward sister at St Stephen's hospital, did a popular stripping nurse.
    No, the problem was really quite easily defined.
    Joan Grimmins.
    She always managed to be hanging around the office at *Dick's*, yet it was very difficult to get her to do any work. Or at least, to get her to act like an employee of Plunkett Strippograms. By being around so much she could quickly push her oar in and get her name down for the simple jobs. But when there was a booking that involved a tedious journey to Theydon Bois, or a particularly unsocial hour, Joan could be trusted to wriggle out of it. The weather that

day would be making her dickie knee play up, or she would have an-outpatient's appointment.

Worse still, she somehow contrived (and it certainly wasn't through the exercise of charm) to have Leofred running errands for her. If he went past a supermarket, she produced a list. If he brought the car to work, he ended up driving her somewhere. Once he wasted the whole of his lunch hour in a post office queue, buying Joan one second class stamp.

'Fire her,' had been Jay's advice. 'She's too fat.' The usually laid-back and easy-going Jay had surprised everyone by taking an active dislike to Joan. Since it was unlikely he had some depth of perception that everyone else lacked, his objection was taken to be a purely aesthetic one.

But Leofred couldn't quite bring himself to do it. He felt too sorry for Joan. If she didn't have the job, what would she have? She didn't appear to have any friends, any social life or interests.

The phone rang again.

'Plunkett Strippograms.'

'Look . . . I know it's short notice, but could you send someone along to a stag do tonight?'

'We'll certainly try, sir. What sort of thing did you have in mind?'

'One of those fat lady-grams. You know, we want someone really big and disgusting to take her clothes off and wobble all over the bridegroom. Really gross him out. Have you got someone like that?'

'Well . . .'

'Some real dog. A real hound . . .'

Leofred hesitated. Did he dare? After all Joan was plain, but was she as bad as all that? And she'd certainly lost a bit of weight since he'd employed her. Perhaps Jay's rude remarks were striking home . . .

Damn it, he was running a business, not a charity. 'Yes,

45

that would be fine. If you could just give me the address . . .'

As soon as he had put the phone down. Joan appeared in the doorway. Her hair was greasy, and in that shapeless coat she really did look . . . well, a bit of a dog.

'Job for you, Joan. Tonight.'

'I can't do one tonight,' she said haughtily, as if this fact were self-evident. 'It's the opening night party.'

'Yes, but . . .' Leofred couldn't bring himself to say *'You're not invited'*. He certainly wasn't going to say that Jay had expressly banned her. ' . . . the guest list's very tight on numbers. And there isn't really anyone else I can send on this one. And . . . well, um, I'm running a business, not a charity.'

Joan chose to ignore that. 'What about Sally?'

'Ah . . . Sally isn't quite what they're looking for. They want someone a bit more . . . rounded.'

'I see,' said Joan fiercely, thumping her handbag down on the desk. 'You want to send me off to some ritual humiliation where a lot of leering men spill beer and take photos of me in my underwear? Is that it?'

'Well, not—'

'I'm not going to do it, do you hear? I refuse to be treated as an object in that way!'

Joan looked as if she might cry. Leofred gave in.

'All right. I'll call them back and see if they'll accept someone a bit slimmer, and if they will, Sally can do it, and I'll go and do her bunnygram for her. But I'll have to go over to her place and pick up the rabbit costume before she goes.'

'In that case . . .' Joan handed Leofred a ticket. 'While you're out you can pick up my dress from the dry cleaners.'

★

Ten forty five p.m.

Heidi and the four-legged, four-armed Jay/Saskia stood at the shrouded bar in *Dick's* club.

'What if nobody comes?' asked Heidi.

'Of course they will!' beamed Jay, who hadn't stopped grinning for at least twelve hours. 'Just cool out, will you? . . . Like the garb, by the way.'

He eyed Heidi's black velvet mini, elbow length black gloves and several kilos of Butler and Wilson costume jewellery with warm approval.

'You don't look so drab yourself.'

Jay was wearing a suit of unashamed vulgarity, in a shiny metallic fabric that caught the light when he moved. 'Great, isn't it? Bit of a one off, really.'

Heidi agreed. 'Only you could wear something like that, Jay . . .'

Eleven fifteen p.m.

Hordes of eager young trendies now packed the as yet unrevealed interior of *Dick's*, waiting for the guest of honour to arrive. A murmur of anticipation swelled up as someone looked out of the window and spotted a large Mercedes drawing up outside the Fulham Road entrance.

Sammi-Dawn Thwort climbed out of the car with some difficulty. She was wearing a very complicated outfit comprising a stretch lurex bodysuit with revealing cut-away holes and a net ballerina's tutu that got stuck half way through the door. Once on the pavement she wobbled dangerously on her six-inch silver stilettos.

Gerry Gyles climbed out after her, brandishing a mobile phone and wearing a suit identical to Jay's.

Sammi paused in the shower of flash bulbs, displaying her best celebrity grin. She waved her silver clutch bag aloft to a chorus of appreciative cheers and whistles. The body glitter smeared liberally into her famous cleavage, caught the light and sent it bouncing back again.

Then Gerry decided enough was enough, and ushered Sammi past the bouncer and into the club.

'Jesus Christ!' said Lez.

Eleven thirty p.m.

' . . . And now,' said Jay Cathcart, positioning himself as far away as possible from Gerry Gyles' suit. 'A big hand please, for Sammi-Dawn Thwort, who is about to do the honours.'

More flash bulbs, more desperate grins from Sammi, as she was handed a pair of scissors.

'*It gives me great pleasure*—' hissed Gerry.

'It gives me great pleasure . . .'

'*To declare this club well and truly open!*'

'To declare this club well and truly open!'

There were cheers as Sammi snipped a silver ribbon, then gasps a amazement as the sheets fell away and *Dick's* club was revealed.

There was no sign of traditional globe lights or wood fittings, or art nouveau. Instead there was a glass floor, lit from beneath by halogen lights which gave the whole room a mysterious pinkish glow. The fittings were all made from dazzling chrome spangled with zircon chips, and the waitresses wore white space cadet uniforms and white roller skates. Instead of one long bar there were several 'service stations' at intervals around the room, where guests could top up their glasses as they passed. No cash would be handed over, instead they would be presented with a computerised account as they left: a ruse to induce rash spending.

A salute of champagne corks was fired, then Sammi-Dawn took her place on the glass podium to 'perform' her new single. Behind the scenes, the club DJ lined up a tape of the recording and tried to pick the right moment to start it. Since he could only see the back of her tutu, he timed it wrong, and Sammi started moving her lips several bars after the song had started.

'Touch my body, gimme a thrill
'I'm a wild beast and I'm ready to kill . . .

The miming left a lot to be desired, but it was no worse than the punters were used to seeing on *Top of the Pops*, and the champagne was flowing at such an indecent rate they were prepared to be more than charitable. Some of them even started joining in the chorus.

' . . . *'Cos I'm feeling sexy, sexy, SEXY!'*

'What d'you think?' Jay hissed to Heidi.

'About what?'

'About the new single.'

Heidi searched for, but could not find the appropriate epithet.

'Well you'd better hope it's a big hit,' said Jay. 'Because if it doesn't start pumping some cash my way, this place is going to have drained itself dry within two months!'

Heidi was appalled. She'd agreed to leave decisions about decor to Jay, but now, looking around at this temple of trendiness, it was apparent that no expense had been spared.

'Jay – for God's sake – how much did all this cost? Jay . . . JAY!'

But he had leapt up onto the podium beside Sammi, who had finished 'singing'. He took the microphone from her.

'A big hand for Sammi-Dawn, please, ladies and gentlemen . . . Thank you . . . and for your information 'I'm feeling sexy' will be released on Rapier Records very shortly, so look out for that one . . .'

Jay waved his hand, and as if by magic Saskia was at his right hand, looking not very bright but very beautiful.

' . . . the disco will be starting shortly, with Rapmaster Funk who has some special house and go-go for you . . . but first I have a small announcement of my own to make . . .

' . . . earlier today Saskia here did me the honour of becoming my wife. So raise your glasses please to the new Mrs Jay Cathcart!'

Eleven forty seven p.m.

Leofred Plunkett was arriving at the annual sales conference of the Sta-Firm Cement Company. He was enveloped from head to toe in a furry rabbit suit, and had a plastic carrot in one hand.

'C'min Bugsy, c'min!' said Ted Dragge, the managing director. He threw one arm round Leofred's neck and hung there drunkenly. ''Sreely nice to see you, sreely nice, isn't it boys.'

He mumbled into Leofred's chest, his beery breath sending a draft through the gap where the bunny head didn't quite meet the bunny body.

In the dismal functions room of a West London hotel, Leofred faced twenty-five plastered cement salesmen. With Ted Dragge clinging somewhere round his knees, he cleared his throat and began to read from his piece of paper, in a squeaky bunny voice.

'Tonight we're here to thank you
With beer and with fags
For selling our cement
You've shifted many bags . . .'

50

There were jeers and cat-calls. A bread roll whistled through the air and hit his plastic nose.

'Get 'em off!' somebody shouted.

'Never mind the telegram – what about the strip!'

'Tell you what boys – let's de-bag her!'

Her?? Then Leofred remembered. He'd never got round to telling them that Sally wasn't coming. He opened his mouth to try and explain but it was too late. Several cement men had already reached the stage and were drowning him out with their lustful howls, their big hands tugging at his furry legs. Ted Dragge, who appeared to have passed out, was trampled in the rush.

It's all her fault, thought Leofred bitterly, as the salesmen wondered what to make of his boxer shorts. Damn Joan Grimmins, damn her!

Twelve seven a.m.

Joan was at that moment experiencing a sensation danger-ously akin to enjoyment.

Of course, she didn't think much of the champagne they'd provided, and they could have put a bit more thought into the buffet, and the music was pretty dreadful, but on the whole she had done the right thing by coming. It had more or less been worth dressing up for. More or less.

Joan had borrowed a dress from her sister-in-law. It was not the sort of thing she normally wore, being made from a shiny pink material with a low cut front. It was also two sizes too small, and squeezing into it had given her curves in all sorts of unaccustomed places. She'd washed her hair and fluffed it up a little, and from somewhere in the depths of a drawer she'd dredged up a grey eyeshadow and a stump end of red lipstick. They were smeared, inexpertly, over her eyes and mouth respectively.

The shiny pink dress seemed to fit in quite well with the general look of the place, and indeed, no-one had tried to stop her when she came in. She'd walked right past Jay Cathcart and he hadn't appeared to recognise her.

Alf the handyman, hadn't recognised her either. He had his eye on her though. He'd stayed on for the duration just in case some of the new electrics went wrong, but he wasn't really feeling at home. There was no-one less than thirty years his junior. Then he saw Joan.

Now there's a good-looking woman, he thought to himself. Bit of flesh on her, going in and out in all the right places. And nice, shiny dark hair. Real hair, not like this spiky stuff most of the girls were wearing. She didn't have a wedding ring on either; that was a good sign . . .

Alf was a widower, and for the last twenty years he'd been saving up for a bungalow in Hastings. He'd got enough to buy one now, with a nice little nest egg left over. All he needed was the right woman, and he'd retire tomorrow . . .

Alf wandered over to Joan, who was standing next to the buffet.

'Thought I'd introduce meself,' he said, extending a hand. 'The name's Alf. And you're the woman of my dreams.'

The fact that she had been cramming crab vol-au-vents into her handbag only made her more interesting.

Joan, on the other hand, was not interested at all. As she held out her hand to shake Alf's, her attention was elsewhere. She was looking over his shoulder at the man who had just walked on. A certain Australian bouncer in search of liquid refreshment.

*

Twelve twenty five a.m.

'Look at them' Ivo said in Heidi's ear. 'Don't they look happy?'

He was pointing at Jay and Saskia, who were wandering around with a newly-wed glow emanating from every orifice.

'Mmmm,' said Heidi, who was more interested in a press scuffle breaking out in another corner of the room.

'I suppose they must have done it some time this morning,' mused Ivo. 'Just sneaked out without telling anyone. And none of us guessed.'

'Well at least it explains why they've been walking around with daft grins on their faces all day,' said Heidi. 'I was wondering whether I should call a doctor.'

'They *do* look happy though, don't they? And sort of . . . different, somehow. It makes you think, doesn't it darling? . . . darling? . . .'

Heidi had escaped to go and oversee a punch-up between the paparazzi and a certain member of parliament. He had been unfortunate enough to be in the same part of the room as Sammi-Dawn Thwort and Maria Meloni when the photographers pounced.

' . . . D'you think we could have a picture of the two of you together girls . . . that's it . . . lovely . . .'

The topless rivals snuggled together as though they were the best of friends.

'Come on girls . . . tiny bit closer . . .' The photographers attempted to fit all four prize breasts into a single frame. This was not easy, as each girl was jostling to stick hers out nearer the questing lens. Their backs arched so much they almost snapped in two.

'That's it, lovely!'

As soon as the photo was finished the girls sprang apart, smiles dissolving into sneers.

'Maria . . . sweetheart . . . d'you think we could get you

with Mr Ryecroft—' The photographers pointed to the MP.
' . . . And d'you think you could sort of lean over him a
bit so yer boobs pop out . . . that's it lovely . . . nearer his
face, sweet'eart . . . that's it, get him on to the floor . . .
lovely . . .'

Twelve forty eight a.m.

Heidi had abandoned the headline-making scene on the
dancefloor and was catching a few quiet moments alone in
the office.

Only a few. She had just put her feet up on the desk
when Lez came in.

'Stay right where you are, mate,' he told her as she
jumped up. 'You're a sight for sore eyes, you really are.'

There was a sharp, explosive little crack as Lez pulled
the tag on a can of lager and emptied it down his throat.
'Here—' he tossed a spare over to Heidi. 'You look as
though you need to wet your tonsils.' He grinned and wiped
his mouth on the back of a brown paw, then rubbed it
down the front of his huge white tuxedo.

'Er . . . Lez . . . shouldn't you be bouncing, or
something?'

'Nah, mate. We're full, so we're not letting anyone else
in. Front door's locked. So Mr Cathcart said why don't you
come upstairs and chuck out anyone who's pissed, so I said
"fair go, sport".'

'Oh, I see. Well, I'll just be going—'

Heidi stood up and walked towards the door, but Lez
blocked her path. Literally.

'Why're you always in such a hurry, eh? Don't go rushing
off, just when you and I've got the opportunity to fool
around. You know I fancy the strides off you, don't you?'

'Well . . .'

Heidi tried to get past, but she didn't try very hard,

and soon found herself being crushed in a hot, muscular embrace. Try as she might, she couldn't prevent tiny currents of electricity running up and down the backs of her legs.

'What's this then?' Lez demanded as his enormous paw delved down the front of her dress. 'Something's rattling down there . . .'

He pulled out a bottle of ZXT 45.

'What the hell are these? You do drugs or something?'

Heidi told him about the pills.

'Streuth!' was all he could say. He began to knead her buttocks with rhythmic, circular movements. Heidi's ankles began to wobble.

The phone rang. In pre-conditioned response, Heidi's right hand disentangled itself and moved towards the receiver.

'Leave it!' ordered Lez. 'Jesus, you yuppies are so wound up all the time! So the phone's ringing. So ignore it. Where were we anyway . . . ?'

Lez's mouth travelled up and down her neck. 'How about you and me giving those pills a little road test?'

Heidi struggled again. 'Really Lez, we shouldn't—'

'LOOSEN UP! Fer Chroist's sake, you want it, I want it, so what have you got to be so uptight about?'

Heidi had to admit that this argument was pretty convincing.

'All you've got to do . . .' murmured Lez, lips inches from hers, 'Is give way to an impulse for a change.'

Heidi stared at his mouth, mesmerised.

'All you've got to do . . . is say one little word. "Yes".'

'Yes,' sighed Heidi.

Lez's mouth lunged towards hers, tongue first. The door opened.

'Anyone in here?' asked Ivo.

*

Twelve fifty nine a.m.

Sammi-Dawn was on her way to the loo. With difficulty. She had drunk seven benedictine and lemonades and was feeling more than a little inebriated. She managed to locate an empty cubicle, but her problems didn't end there. Its sides were very narrow and her net tutu was very wide. Finally she decided to reverse in backwards.

Once in position, she had to find a way of undressing herself. The clinging bodysuit was shaped like a swimsuit and fastened with press-studs between her legs. When she reached forward to undo them, the rigid sides of the tutu got in the way. She held her silver clutch bag between her teeth and tried with both hands. The press-studs flew apart with such force that the clutchbag shot out of her mouth.

'Aw, bleedin 'ell!' screeched Sammi, when she realised she'd peed all over it.

But all was not lost. She staggered out of the ladies again, straight into the the arms of a big, good-looking bloke that she'd had her eye on all evening. She was sure she'd seen him in *Hawaii Five-O*.

'Hoi!' said Lez – for it was he – 'That's a pretty horny get-up you're wearing.'

Sammi blushed and simpered, and ignored the frantic gesticulating from Gerry.

'Tell you what—' Lez held up the bottle of ZXT 45. 'How about doing a little swinging. I've got something really interesting here.'

'Wot – coke?' squeaked Sammi-Dawn.

'Even better. So—' Lez grinned, his eyes boring holes in the front of her body suit. '—How about it?'

*

One a.m.

'Are you sure there was nothing going on?' asked Ivo. He looked suspiciously at the smears of lipstick on Heidi's chin.

'No, no . . .' said Heidi quickly. 'I was just . . . answering the telephone . . . and then . . . Lez came in and said . . . said he had something in his eye and I was just helping him . . . get it out . . . er, when . . . when you came in.'

Why am I lying like this? I'm supposed to be a free agent – Why can't I just come out with it and admit that I've just fallen madly in lust with someone else?

'Well, I'm glad I've got you on your own, darling. I've been meaning to do this for some time, but it's seeing Jay and Saskia together that's finally convinced me.'

Heidi stared at Ivo in horror. He was about to propose. 'No, Ivo, honestly, I'm not . . .'

The door of the office was slightly ajar. Through it, Heidi could see Lez. And Lez was not alone. He had his arms around Sammi-Dawn Thwort and his tongue firmly round her tonsils. She was squirming appreciatively.

Heidi felt her insides go very cold, then her face go very red. What an idiot she'd been! For a moment she had flattered herself that Lez was really interested in her. She'd even been about to turn down Ivo because of him.

'Yes,' she said.

'Pardon?'

'I said YES!' bellowed Heidi. 'That's all I have to do isn't it, say one little word? Well, I'm saying it. Yes.'

Four

The next morning, Sammi-Dawn Thwort and Gerry Gyles were sitting at Gatwick airport, waiting for a flight to Milan.

Gerry was anxious to promote Sammi's career on the continent, where mindless disco music topped all the national charts, so he had arranged a television appearance on Vista Siciliana, a network television company reputedly owned by the Mafia.

Gerry stood up, stretched, and looked at his large, diamond-studded watch.

'I'm just going to pop into the duty free, buy some perfume for Her Indoors. You stay here.'

'Aw!' whined Sammi. 'I wanna buy a—'

'Oh no you don't madam! You can stay right where you are . . .'

Sammi-Dawn was in the dog-house after disappearing from *Dick's* and spending the whole night out at a venue she refused to name. Gerry strolled off to the duty free shop with his cellphone thrust into his back pocket. Sammi sat and sulked behind her wraparound shades.

Gerry was back in a very short time, with a thunderous look on his face and a copy of the *Daily Meteor* in his hand.

'And just what do you call *this?*' he demanded, tapping the front page.

'*PAGE FIVE GIRL TO WED!*' blared the headline. '*My love for Aussi hunk – by topless Sammi*'.

There was a slightly unfocused picture of Sammi at the nightclub, balancing a benedictine and lemonade on her cleavage. She had the sensitivity to blush when she saw it.

'What did you have to go and do that for, you stupid little noodle!' blustered Gerry. 'Spending the night with someone is one thing, but this is not on! Not on at all.'

'Everyone else was gettin' engaged,' whined Sammi. 'I wanted to get engaged too.'

'You can't get engaged to some Australian beach bum! Not at this stage in your career. How's it going to look promotions-wise? You're supposed to have an aura of mystique, not just get picked up by the barman of any old club you walk into!'

'But he's nice and I fancy him,' pouted Sammi. 'Anyway, he's a bouncer, not a barman.'

'Bouncer then.' Gerry was pacing around her in a tight little circle, chewing his thumb and thinking fast. ' . . . Let's see . . . the only thing we can do with this mess is try and turn it to our advantage . . . get some more publicity about you breaking off the engagement . . . then let them see you consoling yourself with someone really worth being seen with . . . right-' He swung round to face Sammi. 'As soon as we get to Italy, you call Crocodile Dundee and tell him it's all off. Meanwhile I'd better start on my contacts.'

With that, he whipped out his phone like a gun from a holster and started to punch in the first number.

At that moment, Heidi Plunkett was just waking and realising with relief that it was a Saturday.

Then she remembered that night clubs were open on

Saturdays and she still had to go to work. She groaned. There hadn't exactly been time for her to acquire a hangover, but her body felt as if it had been soundly beaten all over by a length of bicycle chain.

Heidi stumbled from her bed and into the kitchen to put the kettle on. Then she ran a bath. If she was going to be late in at *Dick's*, she might as well be really late.

When the bath was full to overflowing and the coffee brewed, she tugged the paper from the letterbox, where the paperboy had crammed it with his usual efficiency, and carried it into the bathroom. Perhaps the opening night had been written up . . .

Once immersed, she turned to the Diary page. And dropped her mug of coffee into the water when she saw her own face staring out at her.

'YUPPIE WEDDING OF THE YEAR? Last night, at the opening of a certain Fulham Road night spot, whizz kid billionaire Ivo Cathcart, founder and chairman of the Rapier Group, announced that his second wife was to be the club's part-owner and PR girl, Heidi Plunkett, 26. 'We're thrilled,' said blonde Heidi. And smiling, she admitted that she and her fiance were the perfect yuppie couple.'

'I did not!' yelled Heidi out loud. 'And I'm not blonde – I'm mouse!'

The spilled coffee spread through the bathwater in a muddy brown stain, over her stomach and arms. Heidi looked down at them. Could she really have forgotten all about what happened last night? That wasn't a very good omen. Oh dear, what on earth had she done? . . .

The thirty carat diamond on her left hand winked up at her ominously.

Ivo Cathcart was also working that Saturday morning.

He had telephoned the inner circle of his top executives and dragged them in, grumbling, to a special press conference.

In his office in the Rapier building, his own phone was already ringing insistently. The world at large had heard the news of his engagement and there were calls of congratulation – even one from Downing Street – and numerous enquiries from seekers of wedding trivia.

Ivo handled the situation like the true media-manipulator he was. He fended off the questions with just enough information to keep them interested, then buzzed his secretary, who was also sacrificing her Saturday.

'Jackie . . . telephone Norman Parkinson's office and see if he'll be able to do a set of engagement portraits to hand out to the colour mags. If he's not available, try Lichfield . . . then I want you to book at date at Grosvenor House for the engagement party, as soon as they can do it . . . ask them to quote for three hundred and fifty guests . . . then I want you to contact the top salons: Emmanuel, Cierach, Fratini, and make appointments for each of them in Heidi's name for initial discussions about the dress . . . thanks Jackie.'

Ivo swung his fist high in a salute and let out a little whoop. He sprang the length of the room, the seams of his tailor made wool suit straining over his stocky torso. He considered doing a cartwheel. He felt good. He felt very good.

He fumbled in a drawer and took out a photo of Heidi taken in one of her less stroppy moments. She had a very hostile relationship with the camera. That would have to change. He kissed the photo and stood it on his desk, in exactly the place where the photo of Linda, his ex-wife, used to stand. Then he took a bottle of ZXT 45 out of his pocket and kissed that too, for good measure.

'My little beauties.' he said.

For on his desk sat Paul Latchkey's report, finished at one o'clock that morning, the precise moment he popped the question to Heidi. That had to be a good omen.

The report certainly made very encouraging reading. The statistics were better than any of the experts had predicted they would be. In fact, if this was anything to go by, the women of Britain were more than ready for ZXT 45.

There was a knock on the door. Tony Hendry, head of marketing, and Bob Wylde, Rapier's chief accountant, came in.

'Ready for the press conference, boys-' demanded Ivo loudly, still grinning from ear to ear.

His high spirits only seemed to induce nervousness in his employees.

'Are you quite certain about going ahead with these new, er . . . pills?' asked Tony.

'Quite certain, Tony, quite certain. In fact, young Paul's report is so excellent that I'm going to expand the programme. I'm going to sink a hundred million into the developing, marketing and advertising of ZXT 45, with a view to putting the product on sale sometime early next year.' Ivo rubbed his hands together, as though he was about to tuck into a lavish feast of profits.

'But Ivo . . .' said Bob, wondering how to show concern without sounding like a party pooper, 'That's a . . . sizeable investment—'

'Massive, in fact', said Ivo with satisfaction.

'Massive. Indeed. You know as well as I do that it will use up all of the group's liquid assets, and more besides. You'll have to sell off some of the companies in the group—'

'Not necessary. I've got a much better idea. And if you'll come with me, you'll find out what it is.'

Ivo swaggered down the corridor, head held high, with Hendry and Wylde in his wake like two trainers behind a prize fighter. In one of the conference rooms, Fleet Street's financial correspondents were waiting, yawning, rubbing their stubble and swilling filter coffee.

'Good morning, gentlemen,' said Ivo, taking the stand. 'And may I apologise for dragging you out on a Saturday morning. However, I think your editors will find that it was worth the sacrifice . . .'

One or two of the journalists picked up their pens, or switched on their tapes. All of them continued their absorption of caffeine.

' . . . Rapier will be making use of its new pharmaceutical subsidiary, Star, to introduce a new wonderdrug. Now, the nature of this drug must remain secret for the time being, for obvious reasons, but I am calling this conference today to reveal that we are planning a Rapier stock flotation.'

Heads were raised at this, and coffee cups lowered.

'The sale of shares is planned for the end of October, around six weeks away. Details will be appearing in the press very shortly. Now gentlemen, are there any questions?'

'Would the timing of your engagement have anything to do with this new development?' shouted one hack.

Ivo smiled. 'Are you accusing me of a publicity stunt? Me?'

There was muted laughter.

'Of course, it goes without saying that my business interest and my private life are two separate entities. Let's just say that it's fortunate that the two announcements happen to coincide . . . very fortunate.'

'Now for God's sake, don't mention anything about engagements, or Australians!'

It was Saturday night. Sammi-Dawn Thwort and Gerry

Gyles were arriving at the Vista Siciliana studios in Milan's Corso Magenta. As they stepped out of the car, there was an enthusiastic volley of catcalls from the Italian *ragazzi* outside; gorgeously attired, mirror-shaded and draped over their Vespas. Gerry's rent-a-mob had not been needed here, since the Italians would cheer anything blonde with large breasts.

'*Viva la bionda!*'

'*Viva i meloni incredibili!*'

Sammi and Gerry were placed in the care of the producer of their show, a suave Milanese called Enrico whose clothes made Gerry's look like jumble sale rejects. Sammi's mouth dropped open a little when she saw Enrico's expressive dark eyes and olive skin.

'*Don't even think of it, my girl!*' hissed Gerry.

'Let me explain the set-up,' said Enrico smoothly, in his attractively accented English. 'You know of course, that the variety show goes out live at seven pm—'

'Live?' squawked Sammi.

'My clients do not perform live!' blustered Gerry. 'Not without—'

Enrico just smiled. 'Listen, there's nothing to worry about. Our Italian television is very unsophisticated. This is a simple family show. All Signorina Thwort has to do is stand up and sing a song. What did you have in mind?'

Gerry took out a tape recorder and played a few bars of the 'Sexy' demo. 'Big hit in Britain,' he lied, 'Probably be released over here next month.'

'It's very nice,' said Enrico tactfully. 'But I don't think it is suitable for a family show like ours. Can you do another song?'

Sammi was entering one of her sulks. 'Don't know any,' She said.

'No problem', Enrico was still cheerful. 'Just get out

there and sing whatever you feel like singing. Our musicians will pick up the tune.'

Sammi opened her mouth, but no sound came out. Gerry shrugged, powerless. Enrico smiled and clicked his fingers. *'Giulietta, accompagna Signorina Thwort alla camera d'armadio!'*

Sammi emerged from the wardrobe department a few minutes later dressed as a drum majorette with pom-poms attached to every point of interest. Scowling, she allowed herself to be dragged into the wings to watch the first half of the show.

The overture involved twelve bare-breasted dancers, wading their way through a blitzkrieg of coloured lights and swirling dry ice. Two singers in spandex trousers and sequins screeched their way through a number that was no doubt familiar to the chart-followers in Sicily.

'See,' Gerry whispered to Sammi. 'Nothing to worry about sweet'eart. This lot are awful!'

Family entertainment in Italy was no stranger to nudity. The next act was a stripper who almost drowned in a flood of balloons from the ceiling. She was followed by a team game where housewives ran around the stage in their stockinged feet and threw custard pies at one another.

'You next, please, Signorina Thwort,' said Enrico with a smooth little bow.

'Just get out there and sing!' urged Gerry. 'And don't forget to smile!'

He needn't have worried. As soon as Sammi saw something that looked like a camera, her professional instincts took over. She beamed. She picked up one of the balloons and posed with it, before tossing it into the air. The audience applauded, then settled back expectantly.

Silence.

'*Sing!* mouthed Gerry from the wings. '*SING!*'

Sammi's brain was working as fast as it had ever worked

in its life. What songs did she know? What songs did she like, apart from 'O come, all ye faithful'?

Then she remembered. She had been about six, and her mum had taken her and Daylon to see the circus on Plumstead Common.

'Nelly the elephant packed her trunk
And said goodbye to the circus.
Off she went with a trumpety trump . . .'

The studio band supplied a funky, disco accompaniment. The audience started clapping in time. Sammi found that she was enjoying herself. This was much more fun than miming to a song she didn't know. She opened her mouth wide and bawled at the top of her lungs.

'Oooooooooh! Nelly the Elephant packed her trunk . . .'

She executed a little dance as she sang, kicking up her tasselled boots and jiggling her backside.

The audience roared their appreciation, and when Sammi had finished a dozen or more *ragazzi* mobbed the edge of the stage.

'Brava!'

'Encora!'

Eager Italian hands grabbed at Sammi's ankles, and tried to reach her pom-poms.

'That was excellent,' observed the super-smooth Enrico. 'She chose just the right song for an Italian audience. Don't you think so, Mr Gyles?'

But Gerry was lost in thought. He had just had a very good idea. 'Quick!' he said. 'Quick! Somebody get me a telephone!'

On Monday morning, Leofred Plunkett was the first person to arrive at *Dick's*.

Or so he thought.

He walked into the office to find a woman sitting at his desk. She had her back to him, and appeared to be writing something down.

'Ah, excuse me, can I—'

She turned round.

'Joan! I didn't recognise you!'

'No,' she observed. 'You didn't.'

Joan had obviously been busy with the Carmen rollers over the weekend. Her hair was washed and shiny, and puffed up into a lively froth of curls. She was wearing powder and lipstick, and in place of the shapeless trousers there was a neat blouse and pleated skirt.

You look much nicer than usual, Leofred was about to say, but stopped himself just in time.

'You look very nice,' he said lamely.

Joan let the compliment pass. She produced, out of nowhere, an efficient looking notebook. It had very neat handwriting on it, and things underlined. With a ruler. Leofred experienced a sinking feeling.

'There have been a couple of calls already,' she said. 'Do you want me to go through them?'

'Go on.'

Joan chose to remain seated in *his* chair, at *his* desk, while he stood to attention like an office junior.

' . . . I thought that last one was one you could do. Can you be there for nine o'clock?'

Leofred stared at Joan. 'And what about you? Were you planning to do any work? Or is your purpose purely ornamental?'

'All right, all right!' Joan gave an uncharacteristic little laugh. 'I was only trying to be useful while I was here. And if something suitable comes up, of course I'll do it!'

Leofred cleared his throat and stared pointedly at his chair.

'The coffee machine's just finished. Why don't you go and pour it out?'

Leofred walked slowly over to the machine and laid out two cups. He wondered why he was doing this. Why was he allowing Joan to send him for coffee while she made the decisions about *his* business? He knew he should say something. But what? She would only say she was trying to help.

He would fire her, that's what he would do. He would simply tell her, with no argument—

Joan's voice cut into his executive decision-making. ' . . . And while you're there, pour a cup for Lez, will you. He's been hard at work for an hour, poor thing.'

Leofred allowed himself a measure of spitefulness. 'If it's Lez you've got your eye on, I wouldn't waste your time. He's way out of your league.'

'I wouldn't be too sure of that,' said Joan calmly, stirring her coffee with Leofred's fountain pen. 'I wouldn't be too sure at all.'

A few hours later, the scene in the office had shifted somewhat.

Joan had disappeared, which was just as well, because Leofred now found himself sharing the small room with two giggling temporary secretaries who had appeared out of nowhere and pushed his desk deeper into the recesses of the corner. When Heidi arrived in at half past ten, everything in the room shifted a further twelve inches or so, pinning his body firmly against the wall.

He registered the expression on his sister's face, saw that it read 'BAD MOOD' and hastily buried his head in his customer accounts. Heidi leaned against the door and stared at the two girls, who were flicking rubber bands at one another.

'What are they doing there?' she demanded.

'Mr Cathcart hired us,' said one of them.

'Jay?? What would he do a thing like that for? We've hardly got room to behead a hamster in here as it is! And we certainly haven't got the funds to pay for you. I'm sorry, but you'll have to go.'

The other girl handed her a sealed envelope. Heidi's heart sank when she recognised the Rapier Industries logo.

'*From the office of Ivo Cathcart*' read the letterhead.

'Darling Heidi,
Thought you might need some help in the office this week, as you'll have all the wedding preparations to sort out. I'm sending you two girls from the agency we use, on our account, of course. Don't forget the Industrial Society Dinner tonight – formal, I'm afraid. See you later. Love you.'

'Nice, isn't it,' offered the temp. 'We thought it was really nice, didn't we Jayne?'

Heidi stumbled out of the office before she exploded. She leaned back on the door and closed her eyes. The wedding. The bloody wedding . . .

On the other hand, it wouldn't do her any harm to have someone else answering the phones for a change . . .

A shadow fell over her face. She looked up.

'Hoi!' said Lez. 'Congrats on your engagement, mate. Good on yer!'

'And on yours,' said Heidi sourly.

Lez laughed. 'You don't believe all that shit, do you?'

'Your fiancée certainly seems to.'

'Aw well . . . you know what it's like when you're having a bit of a ding, mate. She just got the wrong end of the stick, that's all. She's a horny sheila an' all that, but she's not like you. Now you're what I call a real woman . . .'

Heidi turned and slammed back into the office before her nervous system could suffer any more damage. 'You might as well stay,' she told the temps. 'Though I don't see why there have to be two of you.'

The reason soon became apparent. Jayne and Cathie were best friends, and they worked for the same agency so that they could go off on jobs together and spend a merry eight hours gossiping and making one another laugh. Usually they were laughing so hard that they couldn't control their snorts in time to pick up a ringing phone, so Heidi ended up taking most of the calls herself.

'. . . No I do not want to be featured in your colour supplement,' she told one Sunday paper. 'And I certainly don't want to contribute a piece called "A Wedding of my Own". Goodbye.'

She started leafing through the club's invoices. Jay had overspent wildly, as she had feared, and the accounts were in a terrible mess. It would take them several months of very high profile promotion to bring in enough money to put them straight.

She looked down at the huge rock on her finger, hesitated for a moment, then dialled Ivo's number.

'Hi, darling' he said, still in irritatingly good spirits. 'I expect you've got a bit more time on your hands now, with two secretaries. That was a good idea of mine, I thought.'

'Well I've had a better idea. Since you're so busy with the new product, and the share offer, and I've got so much on my plate at the club, why don't we just put the wedding back six months or so, then—'

'Out of the question,' said Ivo. 'The arrangements are all under way, and besides, I don't want to wait until next year.'

'But why? I don't see—'

'Sorry darling, no can do.'

He hung up.

'Hey, you're the one that's having the yuppie wedding of the year, aren't you?' demanded Jayne, who had been listening 'I read it in the paper.'

'*I am not a yuppie*'! said Heidi, through gritted teeth.

The temps appeared not to have heard her. 'Hey, Cathie,' snorted Jayne. 'D'you remember Lisa at that place we worked last week? She wasn't a yuppie she was a B.A.R.B.ie – begging for a right bonking! Geddit!'

Snorts of laughter, almost drowning the persistent ringing of the phone.

' . . . and that guy Matthew, the one who drove the Porsche. Well, apparently he was a FUCCER – a fine, up and coming company executive roger! . . .'

More howls.

' . . . Seriously, though, did you see that car of his? *Nice!*. Apparently they used to give them Audi Quattros, but then they changed the bonus scheme . . .'

Heidi put her hands over her ears and started to work through the day's newspapers, which were stacked neatly on her desk.

'*RAPIER TO GO PUBLIC*', was the headline on the front page of the *Financial Times*. 'OCTOBER SHARE OFFER'

'*IVO CATHCART TO WED*' declared the *Daily Mail*.

'*PRINCESS SAMMI?*' said the *Meteor*.

Heidi looked again. There, staring out at her, was a photograph of Sammi-Dawn Thwort with a prince of the realm.

'*This morning Buckingham Palace refused to comment on the rumours of a romance between the young prince and topless model, Sammi-Dawn Thwort (21). But the two lovebirds have been seen out on the town together and a close friend of Sammi's told our reporter: "They are very close. It looks as though wedding bells are on the cards"* . . .'

Heidi looked closer. Sammi's head was higher than the

prince's, and their faces were at a very strange angle, facing away from one another like a push-me-pull-you. Careful inspection revealed that one of Sammi's ears had been chopped off when her photograph had been cut out and superimposed onto an old one of the prince. She had probably been stuck on top of Her Majesty.

Normally Heidi would have laughed at this act of treason, but today she didn't, due to an acute case of Media Overkill Syndrome. She threw the newspapers in the bin and snapped at the temps to answer the phone that had been ringing persistently for two minutes.

'It's one of those dressmakers—' hissed Cathie, covering the mouthpiece. 'The one that did Princess Di! They say you've got an appointment with them tomorrow afternoon. Shall I write it your diary for you?'

'You can't,' said Heidi, without even looking. 'There isn't any more room. I've already got six engagements in tomorrow's space. Tell them to bugger off.'

'Did you know,' offered Jayne helpfully, 'that you can get special supplementary sheets to put in your Organofax, when you need to write in extra appointments? . . . Alex had some of those, didn't she Cath?'

'Yeah, I saw them.'

'Mind you, she really was a yuppie. She had one of those big leather ones . . . have you seen the price of them? . . . I could only afford one of the cheapo plastic ones . . . hey, Cath, d'you now what we are? We're ZINCs – zero income, no children. Geddit?'

'Yeah, and I'll tell you what your brother Mike is . . . he's a YAOW!'

'What's that then?'

'A young anarchist on welfare . . .'

' . . . well . . . hang on, you'd better answer that phone . . . if that's what Mike is, I don't know what Chris is. What d'you reckon Chris is? . . . He's only got a Ford Escort . . .'

Heidi felt a great weariness sweep over her; not physical exhaustion, but a deep weariness of the spirit. She closed her eyes and tried to imagine a place where people weren't stricken with that eighties malaise of labelling one another, where nobody owned a car and nobody had even heard of a Filofax. She found that she couldn't.

'Princess Sammi, eh?' said Tim Goldsmith to Gerry Gyles. 'Brilliant concept. Brilliant. How did you swing it?'

'Contacts,' replied Gerry, tapping his cell phone, 'Contacts.' He scrunched the sleeves of his suit above his elbows with pride. 'And brilliant timing, though I say it myself. Here they come!'

Tim and Gerry were standing in the visitors gallery at Rapier Records (once a cast iron fire escape), watching the first pressings of Sammi-Dawn's single arrive in the packing room. They were being lifted from the conveyor belt in batches of five hundred and sealed into carboard boxes.

Tim leaned over the fire escape and looked closer. 'That's odd! They're useing two different coloured labels. Why would they want to do that?'

'Ah!' said Gerry, delighted that he knew more than Rapier's own man, 'That's because Sammi's recorded two different songs.'

Tim pulled his Beastie Boy cap further down his neck and frowned. 'You've lost me.'

Gerry sighed. 'It's been a sod of a forty-eight hours, I can tell you, getting the second one taped and pressed in time, but since Band Aid these miracles have become possible. As you well know, Tim old son.'

Tim was not happy./ 'Would someone mind telling me what's going on?'

'Come with me, young Tim,' said Gerry generously, who had fast been reaching the conclusion that working in the music business (or 'the biz' as insiders liked to call it) was a bit of a doddle. ' . . . all will be revealed.'

The two of them left the gallery and finished up in the heavily draped, marbled and stippled office of Jay Cathcart. He offered them a choice of mineral waters and the three of them sat down on reproduction Art Deco sofas. Jay eyed Gerry's suede suit with the trained eye of the professional poseur, and decided it was a little bit too Cannes Film Festival.

'Well,' said Gerry. 'We've done it. The singles are in and ready for distribution.'

'We just saw them,' chipped in Tim.

'That's cool,' said Jay 'We want those babies out and on the air pronto, I can tell you.'

'I'll get onto the boys in Distribution right away,' said Tim in an eager tone. He picked up the telephone disguised as an Art Deco ashtray and started dialling.

'Wait, wait . . .' said Jay. 'We need to have a bit of a rap about this first.' He struck a match on the sole of his shoe, blew it out, and tossed it into the ashtray/telephone. 'What we have here are two different hits. We have a disco version of 'Nelly the Elephant', which is for the European markets. And we've got the more sophisticated 'I'm feeling sexy' for the UK. Now, Gerry here is going to handle the the Nelly distrib., since it was all his idea . . .'

'For a percentage,' said Gerry swiftly.

'For a small percentage—'

'And Rapier's going to do the other one?' asked Tim, striking a match on the soul of his Doctor Marten's and missing the ashtray.

'Er . . . not exactly. I'm going to handle it myself. With

74

the help of some distribution experts experienced in tricky situations like this.'

'You mean bribes . . . payola?' Tim looked shocked.

'Look Tim,' said Jay patiently, tossing a lighted match into the mineral water bottle. 'It's important that this record is a big hit; top ten stuff. It's important for Rapier.'

'For Sammi,' said Gerry firmly.

'And for my bank balance. Otherwise we're up shit junction without a credit card, if you get my drift . . . so, I want you to make sure they pack up all the pressings of Sexy and have them delivered to *Dick's* club. My distribution boys are going to handle their business from there. And pack up the master tapes with them and I'll put them in the club safe. I don't want the risk of any pirate tapes floating around. Got that, Tim?'

'So the two releases are going out completely separately? Only—'

'All they've got to do is divide them up. Blue label for Nelly, pink for Sexy. It should be quite simple . . .'

At six thirty that evening, Heidi Plunkett was still at *Dick's* club.

She had agreed to allow a Fleet Street reporter to come to the club and interview her, relenting only because the journalist in question was an anxious junior. A year ago, Heidi had been a reporter herself, and she remembered only too well the demoralisation caused when an interview was refused.

A temporary peace had descended at *Dick's*, which would last until the doors opened to the pleasure seekers at ten o'clock. The giggling temps had gone on their way, and Leofred had disappeared to do a Neil Kinnock-o-gram. Joan was about to step out for a sandwich, putting a raincoat over her low-cut satinette blouse and keeping a weather eye on Lez, who was weight-lifting with crates of Grolsch lager.

The nervous cub feature-writer appeared and fumbled with her notebook and tape-recorder. Heidi watched patiently while the girl discovered that the batteries had run down.

'Got some more somewhere,' she muttered, groping in her bag and spraying Heid's desk with credit card slips, used tissues and hair grips. A new packet of batteries was unearthed, which turned out to be duds.

'I should stick with shorthand if I were you,' said Heidi kindly.

'Right . . . the girl flipped open her notebook, poised her pencil and opened her mouth to fire the first mind-numbingly predictable question.

There was a knock at the door. Alf came in.

''Scuse me, Miss Plunkett, where d'you want us to put this delivery?'

'Delivery? . . . at this time? . . . behind the bar I suppose.'

Alf scratched his head with the leadless pencil he always wore behind his ear as part of his handyman's uniform. 'It's not booze. It's records.'

'*Records?*'

'Thousands of the buggers. From Mr Cathcart. He's sent a note saying they're to be stored here for the time being.'

Heidi asked the reporter to excuse her, and followed Alf out into the club room. She wondered why it was so dark in there, then realised that the subterranean lighting was completely obscured. The glass floor was covered with stacks of cardboard boxes marked *Property of Rapier Recording Ltd*.

Heidi leaned against the wall and uttered a sigh that came from the very soles of her trendy black lace-up boots. If

Jay had walked in at that moment she would have strangled him, if only she could have found the strength.

'I could put them in the office,' suggested Alf.

'Impossible. It's like a Vietnamese boat in there already.'

'The store room, then?'

They looked, but it was stacked to the ceiling with crates of yet-to-be-consumed alcohol. Heidi felt her blood pressure rising. 'What the hell are we going to do with the bloody things? We can't have them cluttering up the place once the club opens! We'd have to turn people away, and that would be disastrous!'

Alf tapped his nose with his pencil. 'I know . . . the van.'

'What van?'

'Me Reliant Robin's gone in for a service, so me brother's lent me his van. He's got a small removals business.'

'Where is it?'

'Parked out the back. We'll have to carry them down the stairs again, I'm afraid.'

'I'll get Lez to give you a hand . . .'

But when he was needed, Lez was nowhere to be found, so Heidi apologised again to the journalist (turning down her offer of help on the grounds that the editor might sue if she hurt herself) and started the laborious process of carrying boxes up and down to the back yard where Alf's van was parked.

'D'you think they'll be okay in here?' Heidi asked, as she and Alf leaned, puffing, against the open door of the van.

Alf struggled to get his breath. 'Don't worry love, they'll be quite safe. I'll padlock the doors and leave the van parked round here until they're needed . . . Mr Cathcart said it was just temporary . . .'

'Is that it, then?' Heidi asked.

'This is the last box,' said Alf, who was still puffing. 'I'll just . . .'

He lifted up the final case of records, and as he did so, his face turned a nasty purpley colour and he started to gasp.

'Alf! Are you all right?' Heidi quickly took the box from him.

'Got a bit of a dickie ticker. Doctor told me to take it easy . . .'

'Why on earth didn't you say so? Just wait there a minute, and I'll go and get you a drink.'

Heidi ran into the club, grabbed a bottle of brandy, ran down to Alf, was assured he'd be all right if he took things gently for a while, ran into the club again and tripped over Lez.

'And where the hell have *you* been?' she demanded.

'Fair go, mate! I was only in the ruddy toilet! Isn't a bloke allowed to take a—'

'All right, all right!'

'Where's the ruddy fire, anyway?'

'Never mind! It's a long story and I don't have the time!'

Heide pushed past Lez and collapsed, panting, on top of the reporter, who was waiting in the office with her pencil still poised.

'Sorry . . . it's been one of those days. You were saying? . . .'

She sleep-talked her way through the questions about her past career and the stone on her engagement ring and how many guests would be attending the wedding.

'Do you mind telling me how you feel about the timing of the wedding?'

The journalist's voice took on a harder edge, one that Heidi recognised only too well. It meant that she had been told by her editor to ask this question, and she was girding herself with the necessary professional ruthlessness.

'I'm sorry?'

'At a press conference Mr Cathcart admitted that chosing this moment to announce the engagement was a publicity stunt to draw attention to his business ventures. I wondered how you felt about that?'

Heidi felt sick. And she felt tired, crushingly tired. She stood up. 'I'm sorry, but I'll have to end the interview there . . . have to go . . . a dinner engagement . . .'

She bundled the accoutrements of twentieth century life into her bag and stumbled out of the office. Ten minutes later she found herself wandering around Redcliffe Square in the dark, unable to remember where she was going.

This is it, she told herself. *It's finally happened to me. I'm having a nervous breakdown . . .*

A telephone rang shrilly, making her jump out of her skin. She rushed to answer it, then realised that it was a telephone inside the house that she was passing, and nothing to do with her at all. She didn't have to worry about it. She leaned against a lamp-post and closed her eyes, to be woken, seemingly hours later, by the high-pitched bleeping of her radio-pager, still strapped to her belt.

It was Ivo, she knew it instinctively. He would be ringing to find out why she was late home. They were going out that night, she remembered, to a black tie dinner.

But I can't! My dress is at the cleaners . . .

The fact that she had other dresses was quite obscured by this sudden obsession with getting herself to the dry cleaners, as she had meant to do two hours ago. She broke into a run, and kept on running for half a mile down the Fulham Road until she reached the welcoming portals of Eezi-Kleen Limited.

Heidi ran inside. 'I'm not too late, am I?' she almost shouted.

'That depends, madam. Where are you going?'

'Where am I *going?*' She opened her eyes and looked around her. The room swam into focus for the first time. Posters of sunlit scenes. Rows of brightly coloured brochures. She had run into the travel agents by mistake.

'Did you have anywhere in mind, madam?'

'Oh . . . anywhere. As long as it's soon.'

An hour later, still unable to get a reply from Heidi's pager, Ivo Cathcart left the Industrial Society Dinner and two hundred tuxedo-clad businessmen, and told his chauffeur to drive him home.

As the Bentley came to a halt in the Knightsbridge mews, he noticed that there were no lights on in either house, but this filled him with irritation rather than foreboding. He was far too 'up' to feel foreboding. But on the other hand his time was mapped out like a military campaign at the moment, and it was rather exasperating to have to chase around after Hiedi.

'Darling?' he called, banging on her front door.

There was no reply. Perhaps she was still at the club, after all, and the ignorant Australian oik who answered the phone was just imaginging that she had left hours ago . . . or could he have been covering up for something? . . .

Ivo suddenly remembered what the Australian looked like, and morbid imaginings sprang to life in his brain. No wonder she had been behaving so oddly lately. She was having an affair, the little . . .

Unlocking the front door with the spare key she kept under a flower tub, he bounded up the stairs, three steps at a time and flung open the bedroom door.

Nothing. The whole room had an unnatural tidiness. The bed was made, for once.

And at its centre, something gleamed. The ring.

Ivo picked it up, disbelieving. Then he read the note.
'*Ivo, I can't marry you. I've gone away. H.*'

At *Dick's* club, the doors were about to open to admit the public.

The pre-business hush of a few hours earlier had intensified to an uncanny near silence; the calm before the storm. In the bar, rows of freshly polished glasses gleamed in readiness under the pink halogen lights, and the diamante studded chrome winked and sparkled. The waitresses slid about the room on their roller skates, depositing bowls of cashew nuts and exchanging the odd comment in low voices.

There was only one light on in the office. Joan Grimmins was using it to read a racy novel with a burning house and a heaving bosom on its cover.

The phone rang.

'Plunkett Strippograms . . .' said Joan, in a pleasant, receptionist's voice. When she had taken the message and hung up the phone she smoothed her sleek brunette curls and inspected her fingernails, painted with 'Coral Lagoon'.

There were footsteps behind her, and a pair of hands planted themselves on her shoulders.

''Ello darling,' wheezed Alf. 'You're looking smashing, if you don't mind me saying so.'

'I do, as a matter of fact,' replied Joan, snatching an emery board from her handbag and filing furiously at her coral fingertips. Her prim tone did not discourage Alf, who was eyeing her décolletage with a rising flush on his wrinkled cheeks.

'Aw, come on now, don't be shy! Give us a kiss!'

Joan tried to duck the advance, but she hadn't allowed for the fact that Alf was in the grip of an unreasonable passion. She found herself pinned against the edge of Leo-fred's desk, with Alf almost on top of her.

'I'm afraid you don't understand,' she said, doing her best to stop the laying on of hands that was threatening her ample bosom. 'I'm really not interested.'

'Aw, go on!' Alf increased his efforts, somehow squeezing one shrunken leg between Joan's generously proportioned two. 'I've got a lovely bungalow in Hastings! And you're not getting any younger!'

Joan rallied at this, and in the ensuing struggle managed to get the advantage and tip Alf over. He fell heavily against the side of the desk and rolled onto his back. His face had turned a strange shade of mauve, and he was gurgling.

The gurgling stopped.

'Where's the ruddy fire?' asked Lez, bursting into the room with a cheerful smile on his face. 'Chroist alive! What's up with him?'

Joan looked at Lez, then at Alf, then at Lez again.

'I think he's dead.'

Five

At the end of the Kings Road, not far from the World's End, was a select establishment called *Body Beautiful*. Its aim was to take a lot of money from vain people in return for letting them torture themselves with bits of chrome and leather in the hope that they could change the shape that God had given them.

Gerry Gyles' Mercedes drew up outside, smack in the middle of a double yellow line, and he jumped out, whistling cheerfully.

'Morning Corinne!' he said to the girl on reception.

'Morning Mr Gyles' she replied, shivering in her skimpy aerobics costume. 'What's it going to be this morning – sauna? Aromatherapy? Massage?'

'Just the work-out, please,' said Gerry, signing the members' book. He went into the changing room and exchanged his linen suit for a running vest, a pair of American-style sweat pants and a heavy leather body belt. Then he set off for the main gym, carrying his cell-phone in one hand.

He jumped onto the exercise bike for a warm up, and as his legs whirred busily, his fingers punched his secretary's number into the phone.

'Hello Sally . . . yes . . . I'm on 243 7821. I'll be on this number for an hour or so . . . after that you'll be able to get me on the car phone – that's 240 7357 . . . yes, that's right . . . then I'll be at Rapier Records for a while, so you'll be able to reach me on their number, which is 221 9835 . . .'

Gerry tucked the phone into his belt and began to pedal in earnest, making little blowing shapes with his mouth like a distressed goldfish. The long, low-ceilinged room was tense with the hush of concentration, broken only by the occasional grunt. Serious young women in wrestling boots and T-shirts with slogans saying 'Strength Athlete' or 'Nautilus USA', watched their reflections on the floor-to-ceiling mirrors. There was no question of them smiling at their image's struggle to raise the shiny chrome dumb-bells above their heads. Those who had a sense of humour – and there weren't many – left it at the door of the gym.

Gerry had just started on a series of bench presses using his telephone as a weight, when Tim Goldsmith walked in.

'Tim, glad you could join me old son! I thought this would be as good a place as any for us to have a bit of a rabbit. Going to pump a bit of iron, are you?'

Denuded of his forage cap and American Classics Levis, Tim Goldsmith looked like the sort of man who had sand kicked in his face on the beach. His skinny legs protruded from shapeless shorts, purple and pimply like a couple of chicken pieces in a supermarket freezer section.

Tim examined the equipment dubiously. 'Er . . . how d'you drive these things, Gerry?'

'Nothing to it . . .' Gerry came to his assistance. 'Why don't you start with the adductor?' He led Tim to something resembling a leather guillotine, complete with ropes and pulleys. 'Ninety pounds ought to do to start you off.' He adjusted the weight.

'Ninety??'

'Not much, I'll grant you, but if you stick at it, you'll soon be on a hundred and fifty.'

Gerry positioned himself opposite the machine so that he could swing his dumb-bells and carry on a conversation with Tim at the same time.

'I'd say we've got Sammi's career off to a flying start, wouldn't you, young Tim?'

Tim groaned in agreement, his eyes bulging.

'Keep your legs straight . . . that's better . . . and try holding it there for a few seconds . . . yes, I'm well pleased. And with all this publicity the tabloids have been giving her . . .'

Gerry's cellphone rang, so he exchanged it for one of the dumb-bells.

'That was a producer from TV Mayhem,' he said with satisfaction, going from phone to dumb-bell again. 'They want Sammi-Dawn for 'Celebrity Undies' . . . My strategy is to keep the press guessing. Beat them at their own game, I say. Just as this royal story's getting a bit hot, we'll move her on elsewhere. I thought an ageing rock star, someone about fifty? What d'you reckon?'

'Good . . . idea,' puffed Tim.

'Maybe you could take care of that one for me, Tim? Use your contacts in the biz? . . .'

Tim did his best to nod.

'The other idea I wanted to knock about is albums. I don't know how you feel about it your end, Tim, but I thought it might be nice to try and do an Xmas album. We could whizz it out in time for the Xmas market. Wouldn't take long to do a few cover versions of all the old favourites . . . what d'you think, Tim?'

'Mmmm.'

'We could have Sammi on the sleeve, wearing nothing but a Santa hat. The punters'd love that. And we could give it a catchy sort of title . . . "Sammi Cashes In" . . . or how about "Rocking all the way to the Bank"? . . .'

The doors of the gym swung open and Jay Cathcart came in. Saskia trailed a few yards behind, looking nervous.

'Jay, my son!' Gerry demonstrated his muscles. 'Come for a work-out?'

Jay's face was like thunder. 'We've got a problem,' he said, thrusting his hands deep into his pockets. 'We've got a mega-problem. In fact, we are talking crisis here.'

Gerry lowered his dumb-bell to half mast as a sign of respect. 'What's happened?'

'The pressings of Sammi's single. They've disappeared.'

There was a loud clang as Tim Goldsmith dropped his ninety pounds on the floor.

'What . . . all of them?'

'All of them.'

Heidi Plunkett opened her eyes and wondered why she had been sleeping in a cupboard.

Or perhaps she was in a drawer. She reached up and felt four panelled wooden sides, enclosing her. It was very dark, very hot and very stuffy. Somewhere in the background there was a loud screeching sound, like a tom-cat being castrated. That was odd. She didn't have a cat, and neither did any of her neighbours.

Then she remembered. She wasn't in Knightsbridge. And this wasn't a wardrobe, or a chest of drawers, it was a boat.

So much for snap decisions, she thought. At the end of her bunk were the clothes she had been wearing at the office the day before. Beside her bed was her bucket bag, containing Organofax, aircall bleeper, and the remote message retriever for her answering machine. All the trappings of her life were there, everything was exactly the same. Except now she was somewhere off the south west coast of Turkey.

'Turkey's our top destination this year.' That was what the clerk in the travel agency had told her, with a winning smile. 'And the climate's gorgeous in late September . . .'

'Fine . . .' Heidi had said. 'Turkey will be fine.'

'Sunworld do a nice package on those schooners, cruising round the coast. Very popular with people your age. Would you like me to check? . . . Oh dear, it looks like our only free booking is a last minute cancellation, and that's leaving this evening—'

'Fine,' said Heidi. 'That'll do.'

Like a sleepwalker she'd hailed a taxi and asked it to wait while she ran into her house, flung a few resort clothes into a bag and scribbled a few words to Ivo. Then the cab had taken her to Gatwick just in time to catch the night flight to Izmir.

On the aeroplane, after a couple of scotches and unmelt-able ice from a plastic cup, she'd emerged from her trance long enough to decide that possibly this wasn't such a good idea after all. She'd flagged down a stewardess.

'Can you ask the pilot to stop please?' she'd burbled. 'I want to get off!'

The stewardess had given her a pitying smile and another double scotch.

By the time they landed at Izmir she was plastered, and allowed herself to be guided by the rep. to a minibus which took her and a very odd assortment of holiday makers to the coast, where their boat was waiting for them. Heidi snored loudly all the way, while the others sat in embarrassed silence.

She had a vague recollection of being introduced to her fellow cruisers, and the Turkish crew, and drinking rather a lot of nasty Turkish white wine before being led to her cabin and slotted into her bunk.

The caterwauling noise was still audible. Heidi climbed down from her bunk and did her best to clothe herself, though she couldn't work out where the light switch was, if it existed. Dressed in the bottom half of her suit, a back-to-front sweater and flip-flops, she stumbled out of her cabin and onto the fore-deck.

The sun was just rising, streaking the sky with rich shades of rose and violet, which made a gleam of colour on the inky water. Silhouetted against the sky was a minaret, with the muezzin calling the faithful to prayer.

So that's what all the row was about, thought Heidi. *Bloody foreigners . . .*

There was one other voyager already on deck, a man who Heidi vaguely remembered was called Derek. He wore a pair of polyester slacks, white deck shoes and a selection of gold chains round his neck. He looked down at the sea, slapping against the sides of their boat, and then up at the horizon.

'Dawn,' he said.

'Oh God,' said Heidi.

'I had a girlfriend called Dawn once,' mused Derek. 'A right little goer.'

Heidi could not think of an appropriate rejoinder, so she examined the boat instead. It looked bigger by daylight, about a hundred feet long, and spotlessly clean, every piece of varnished wood and brass sparkling. At the bow end there was a dining table shaded by an awning, and at the stern a large sun deck with coloured loungers. A small rowing boat and two windsurfers were strapped onto the sides of the boat.

'Smart, isn't she?' said Derek proudly, as if it had been his idea to build it. 'Just about the best one in this harbour, I reckon.'

The two of them scanned the jetty to confirm this fact, and their gazes came to rest simultaneously on a boat moored on their starboard side. It was bigger than theirs, and whiter, and had two sun-decks and a much fancier awning. The holiday makers on board were dressed in formal yachting gear, with white ducks and nautical caps and a lot of blue and white stripes.

'Flash bastards!' muttered Derek. He took a pair of opera glasses out of his pocket and viewed the opposition.

'Germans!' he exclaimed. 'They're bloody Krauts, aren't they! Bastards!'

He leaned over the railing and cupped his hands over his mouth. 'OI!' he shouted, his voice ringing out over the tranquil bay. 'YOU BOMBED MY GRANDMOTHER'S CHIP SHOP!'

The crew were in evidence now, scurrying barefoot about the decks, winding the ropes into tidy coils and checking the moorings.

'We'll be off soon, I reckon,' said Derek sagely. 'They'll be pulling up the ruddy anchor in a minute, I'll bet you.'

'Oh dear,' said Heidi, beginning a pre-programmed rummage in her handbag, then remembering that it was in the cabin. 'I wanted to try and find a phone. I really ought to ring my office.'

Derek gave her a sidelong look, but made no comment. 'Oh look, here come the others! Must be time for a spot of grub.'

The other eight passengers were inching their way cautiously to the front of the boat, looking white and fragile ii the strong sun.

'Good job we got through the introductions last night, eh?' said Derek, rubbing his hands in a hearty fashion. 'That way we already know each other's names.'

Heidi had been too drunk to absorb this vital information, so she sat down at the table and kept silent until she had worked out who everyone was. There was a pair of newly weds called Alan and Jo, who never spoke except to one another, two lively post-graduate students called Michael and Jim, a lady academic with a wild look in her eye who talked a lot about sex and drugs in the sixties, and her friend who ran a chain of hairdressing salons. The fourth pair were two gormless brothers called Will and Phil who ran an off-licence in Somerset and talked a lot about motorbikes.

'Looks like everyone knew someone before they came, except you and me,' Derek observed to Heidi. 'Never mind, we'll have to look out for one another, eh?'

Heidi said nothing, concentrating on spreading her butter before it turned liquid in the sun.

'Mind you . . . I shouldn't think you girls'll be lonely long with all those hunky Turks around. Looks like some-one's got to work already . . .'

He pointed at Hazel, the lady don, who had produced a Turkish-English dictionary from her bag and was engaging the first mate in a laborious conversation. The dictionary was handed to and fro at regular intervals as each pointed out the translation of the words.

'You are *excellent?*' queried the Turk, looking at the translation with a puzzled expression.

'No, no, not "excellent", *excited*. I am *excited* to be in Turkey.'

The Turkish word for 'excited' had heavily sexual over-tones, and the first mate returned to the galley licking his lips and turning back to leer at Hazel. 'Tonight!' he shouted. 'Tonight you very excited!'

After the breakfast dishes had been carried into the hot, subterranean hole of the galley, the engine started to throb and the anchor chain was slowly winched up from the harbour floor. Heidi's fellow passengers flocked onto the sun-deck with towels, sun-tan oil and brain-numbing paper-back books. They took up position on the loungers, looking out eagerly towards the horizon as they oiled their pink shoulders.

Only Heidi hung back, overcome by panic. She stumbled into the saloon, desperately trying to catch the attention of the crew. 'Er, excuse me, please, you've got to stop . . .'

The chef, standing behind the bar, went on polishing glasses stonily.

Then Heidi caught sight of Rehjet, the on board rep. employed by Sunworld. He was a slender, sultry-eyed youth who was studying English at the University of Istanbul. Rehjet kept himself slightly apart from the other Turks, sitting at the table and sipping slowly from a glass of raki and water.

'Yes?' he said, raising one eyebrow as Heidi approached. He had been working the same stretch of coast since June, and the jaded expression on his face made it clear that there were no bizarre aberrations of tourist behaviour that he had not yet witnessed.

'Can I get off please?' asked Heidi. 'I need to make a phone call.'

Rehjet just looked her up and down, gave a short laugh and started to pick his teeth.

Heidi looked down at her little white legs and felt a blush of furious self-consciousness wash over her face. 'You don't understand, I'm afraid . . . I've got a business to run, and I've just gone and walked out on it . . . I ought at least to let them know where I am . . . and I was supposed to be getting married and I just ran off without explaining properly—'

'Forget it,' said Rehjet with his faintly American accent. 'We've got a timetable we must keep up with or I get in trouble with the tour company.' He made a cutting gesture across his throat. 'Anyway, even if we did turn back, you wouldn't be able to telephone from Fethiye. It's a very small place; no international telephones. It's difficult for me to telephone to my family in Istanbul.'

'But surely . . . I mean, when *will* I be able to make a call?'

Rehjet just shrugged and returned to his raki.

Heidi went down into her cabin, but with the engine running it was unbearably hot in there and she was forced up on deck for air. The boat was surging forward into the open sea now, sending up a cloud of spray around the bow. And her compatriots were getting nicely primed to the holiday mood, cracking open endless cans of Turkish beer, pretending to throw one another overboard or walk the plank. Still clutching her bag of valuables, Heidi made her way to an empty lounger next to Colin and Jo. She lay back, resigned, and covered her face with a towel to keep off the fierce Aegean sun.

A few yards away, Hazel and the randy first mate Veysel, were still tussling with the dictionary.

'Later . . .' growled Veysel. 'Later you and me have much rum!'

'Rum?' There was a frantic flicking through the dictionary pages. 'Rum . . . drink?'

'No, no, no drink. Rum . . . rum . . .' Veysel's *mot juste* was on the tip of his tongue.

'Rumba? Rumble? Rummage? . . .'

'Rumpy-pumpy?' suggested Heidi, without opening her eyes.

'Ah yes!' Veysel remembered the word he had heard British tourists using. 'Tonight there will be much rumpy-pumpy!'

In *Dick's* club at that moment, there was much consternation.

The mercy dash staged by Jay (complete with Saskia), Gerry and Tim had been foiled by an enormous yellow Denver boot on the wheel of Gerry's Mercedes. Jay did not have his car with him, and passing cabbies cocked a snook – rudely – at the suggestion that they convey the passengers a mere few hundred yards to the Fulham Road. They were left with the horrific alternative of walking. Jay and Saskia leaned on one another all the way like the walking wounded, while Gerry and Tim affected nonchalance, as though they were travelling this way by choice, not because their vehicle was clamped.

Lez, who had spent a quiet morning flattening used lager cans and singing 'Tie me kangaroo down, sport', was seized and interrogated.

'The records!' shrieked Gerry 'What happened to the bloody records?'

'Er, excuse me,' said Leofred, emerging from the back office when he heard the commotion, 'I think you ought to—'

'Hang tough there a minute, Leof,' said Jay, blocking the doorway to the office. 'We're having to get a bit heavy. Talking major probs here.'

'But—'

'Listen,' said Gerry, putting a hand on Lez's shoulder, feeling the muscles and thinking better of it. 'Were you here in the club last night?'

'Yeah, that's right mate. I expect you've heard about what happened to old Alf?'

'Alf? What's he got to do with it?'

'He only died, mate! Had a heart attack and popped off this earthly coil, right here in this club.'

There was a brief, respectful silence but Lez's interrogators were not distracted for long.

'Well, that's terrible, he was a nice old bloke . . . where

were we? Yes . . . so if you were here last night, you'll know what happened to the discs?'

'Discs? What discs, mate?'

'The ones that were delivered to the club last night! In boxes! You can't have missed them!'

'Excuse me,' said Leofred, 'I don't think—'

'Hey! Take five, will you Leof!' snapped Jay, hugging Saskia to him even tighter. 'This is important.'

'What time was it?' asked Lez.

'About seven.'

'Let's see now . . .' Lez scratched the hairs on his naked chest. 'I think I missed that. See, I was in the toilet.'

'In the *toilet?*'

'Fair go, sport.!. Surely a bloke's allowed to sit in the dunny once in a while?'

'But you must have seen something!' Gerry was desperate, seeing his twenty per cent commission on Sammi's profits disappearing, literally, down the pan. 'You can't have missed it all!'

'Truth is, I'd had one or two vindaloos the night before so . . . I did hear some thumping and banging about, but when I came out it was all over and no-one would tell me what was bloody going on.'

'So . . .' Jay sighed. 'Who else was here at the time?'

'Reckon it was just me and Alf—'

'Some witness!' sighed Gerry.

' . . . and Heidi, of course. She was talking to some journo sheila. Nice little redhead, I recall, with massive—'

'So Heidi would know where the records are?' There were smiles of relief all round. 'So it's simple then. As long as they haven't been nicked, all we have to do is ask Heidi where the singles are.'

'Ah . . . the thing is . . .' Leofred squeezed round Jay and Saskia. 'What I was going to tell you is that you can't. Because she – Heidi – she's gone.'

94

'Gone? You don't mean another heart attack?'

'No, she's gone away.' All eyes were on Leofred now, and he turned red, as though it were all his fault. 'Ivo phoned this morning. He said she'd gone away, but he had no idea where.'

There was a stunned silence. Eventually Saskia, who seemingly hadn't uttered in public for weeks, spoke. 'But she's *engaged!*'

'Okay, guys, don't panic!' said Jay with authority. 'First, we'll search the place from top to bottom. Then if all else fails, I'll call my brother. He'll be able to find Heidi. He can get anything done . . . otherwise, why bother being loaded with cash?'

Unable to find fault with this philosophy, the search party set out, but there were not many places several thousand records could be concealed. Everything was as it had been, inside and out, except for a battered old transit van parked in the yard, which Jay decided they ought to set fire to for being an unaesthetic object. Leofred volunteered to have the police tow it away, instead.

'I know!' said Tim Goldsmith. 'I've had a brainwave. Why don't we just press some more discs?'

Jay gave him a look of withering scorn. 'One: because it's too expensive. Two: the master was with the first pressings, because I wanted to keep it in the safe.'

'Couldn't Sammi re-record . . .' Tim's voice tailed away as he realised this option was too horrific to contemplate.

'I'll make that phone call,' said Jay.

When Ivo Cathcart received the phone call, he was in no mood to humour his disaster-prone younger brother.

'No, I will *not* employ private detectives in every country in the world to try to get her back. She's a free agent, and

if she chooses to walk out on me that's her loss isn't it . . .
no, I don't care about where your fucking records have got
to . . . your business may well be facing "mega-debts", but
I can assure you it's a Sunday school outing compared with
what's going on here . . . you'll have to find her
yourself . . . goodbye, Jay! . . . I said "goodbye".'

Ivo put the receiver back in its cradle and looked up at
the circle of faces around his desk, who were all pretending
hard that they hadn't been listening in. Rapier's financial
and marketing gurus were gathered in their supremo's office
for a crisis meeting about the new product.

'So, David,' said Ivo grimly, addressing the head of
Research and Development. 'Tell me the bad news again.'

'We've hit a major drawback in the field trials, I'm afraid.
While most of the consumers who used ZXT 45 enjoyed
the initial effects, they all complained of unpleasant side
effects the next morning.'

'Side effects?' asked Ivo, thinking of his home experiment
with the drug.

'Along the lines of a severe, debilitating hangover, with
partial memory loss of the events immediately prior to use.
Obviously it's out of the question for us to put the drug on
the market in its current form. We're satisfied that there
are no long-term effects, but consumers simply won't want
to use a drug that—'

'Obviously, obviously,' said Ivo, jumping up from his
desk and pacing around the room with his hands in his
pockets. 'In your opinion, David, how long will it take to
iron out this problem?'

'We're hopeful that it won't take more than a few
months.'

'*Months!*' barked Ivo. 'Listen, man, we do not have
months! The share offer is only four weeks away, and we'd
scheduled the product launch to co-incide!'

'Ideally, yes, but—'

'There's nothing ideal about this!' Ivo swung round on one heel and fixed his gaze in the hapless David. His piggy face was an ugly shade of scarlet. 'Just tell me, if money were no object, if your boys were working round the clock, seven days a week, could you iron out the problems and have the product ready, and packaged in four weeks.'

'Just about, I suppose.'

'Right, that's settled then. We'll do it.'

'But Ivo,' remonstrated Bob Wylde, his chief accountant, 'Aren't you going to put the whole enterprise, the whole company at risk, by rushing into this? Shouldn't we leave the product launch until after the share offer—'

'Can't afford to,' snapped Ivo. 'We desperately need the press coverage to boost the share sale. And since I'm no longer Bridegroom of the Year, I need all the publicity I can get.'

'But the capital outlay required to rush this thing through . . . it'll dry up all our reserves . . . supposing the share offer's undersubscribed—'

'It'll never happen! The market's booming! The public'll be fighting for the shares.'

'Even so, the drug will be without any sort of track record . . .'

Ivo ignored all the objections. 'Let's push on, shall we? The publicity campaign. I thought we could have millions of pink balloons, in the shape of suppositories, released over London, and a plane flying over with a banner saying "ARE YOU FEELING SEXY?". What d'you think?'

There was an embarrassed silence.

'Tasteless?'

'Well, er, no . . .'

'Of course it's tasteless, damn it! But tasteless is effective, right? Look at the Sex Pistols! . . . right, next we have to finalise a brand name for ZXT 45? Over to our marketing men, I think. Paul?'

'Well!' gushed Paul Latchkey, dropping his notes in his eagerness to be teacher's pet. 'We've been working on this for a while now, and our research shows that the public won't go for anything too jokey, or risqué . . .'

'Pity,' said Ivo.

'What we need is a name that the consumer will recognise as a patented drug, that is at the same time suggestive . . . er, of its purpose.'

'Any ideas?' offered Ivo.

'*Bonkatron?*' suggested someone.

'Too tabloid.'

'How about *Aphrofen?*'

'Too racial . . .'

Eventually the concensus rested on *Contracon*, and the gurus departed quiescent, if uneasy.

As soon as they had left the office, Ivo's confidence left him in a rush, like air leaving a deflating balloon. The high colour drained from his face and he slumped over his desk for some time, exhausted.

Then he picked up the phone and dialled a number from memory. There were two clicks, followed by a familiar message.

'This is 584 2323. Sorry not to be here to take your call. Please speak after the tone.'

'Heidi . . . I know you won't be there, but just in case you call your machine to get the messages . . . oh shit, look . . . please come back, darling. You can forget about the wedding and everything, but just come back . . . Please.'

Nightfall in Marmaris.

Heidi was still suffering from a sense of displacement, but she had no intention of returning to England.

The Sunworld boat was bobbing in the dark water of the harbour. Only a few yards away, the lights of the busy little port winked and sparkled; exciting, foreign, liberating. On board the boat, the dinner conversation was of company cars, mortgage rates and Mrs Thatcher's last election victory. Will and Phil chipped in with the occasional piece of information about motorbikes.

Heidi had been quiet and subdued all day, and her fellow sailors were giving her a wide berth, concluding that she was stand-offish or anti-social, or both. Only the good-natured Derek persisted, chatting about his dry-cleaning business in Harpenden and his previous holiday in Ibiza, and the suburban cricket club he belonged to. He didn't ask her about her own life, but when she sat on the deck staring out at the horizon he watched her with a sage expression, his eyes narrowed in his chubby face.

The ten of them feasted on octopus and meatballs, and after a dozen bottles of Turkish rosé had been consumed, the paean to Thatcher's Britain blurred into noisy and rather free performances of the Monty Python parrot sketch.

' . . . *It is an ex-parrot, it is no more* . . .' chortled Michael, collapsing with laughter and knocking half a bottle of wine over Jim.

' . . . D'you remember that Honda 750 we had a go on down in Yeovil . . . d'you remember that, Phil?'

' . . . Yeah . . . magic, Will.'

' . . . *It has popped its clogs, it has snuffed it* . . . hey, wait a minute, where's everyone gone? . . .'

'Everyone' had gone up onto the roof of the saloon, overlooking the sun-deck and was boogying around to a Madonna tape that somebody had slotted into the boat's makeshift stereo. The Turkish crew, taking the lewd movements of hips and groin rather too literally, were blundering among the dancers in a fever of lust, fondling passing expanses of naked flesh. A Turkish fishing boat moored fifty yards away decided to start up a rival party, and soon there was loud Turkish music vying with Madonna. The Turkish fishermen flashed their spotlights across the water, then turned them on themselves to illuminate their prowess at belly-dancing.

A roar went up from the British contingent and they took up the challenge; finding pocket torches for an impromptu light show as they stripped their midriffs and made a brave attempt at the national dance.

'Not joining in?'

Derek was at Heidi's elbow as she sat, arms around knees, on the sun-deck, watching the revelry.

Heidi shook her head.

'I say, get a load of those two!'

'Who?' Heidi squinted in the darkness.

'Hazel and Veysel, the odd couple of the century.'

The doyenne of the South Bank Polytechnic and the boat's first mate were engaging in Sex by Dictionary. The small Collins Edition was being passed to and fro at a furious rate, steam practically rising from its pages.

' . . . I . . . ' (Flick, flick) 'I . . . fumble your apples . . . '

'You can't relax, can you?' observed Derek. 'You're as wound up as when you got on that plane. What's wrong?'

'I think I came to the wrong place.'

Derek looked hurt.

'No, I mean..it's very nice here, it's a lovely place for a holiday . . . but its too close to home.'

'I would have thought a couple of thousand miles was far enough for most people. Anyway, you're the one who keeps wanting to find a bloody phone all the time!'

'I know.' Heidi gave him a wry smile. 'That's because I haven't switched off yet. And I don't seem to be able to switch off while there are so many reminders of our own culture . . . '

On the roof above them, the happy holiday-makers were singing 'Land of Hope and Glory', with the exception of mousy Colin and Jo, who were playing Trivial Pursuit.

'I went to Japan once,' said Heidi. 'When I wanted to get away from it all.'

'And did it work?'

Heidi laughed. 'The culture shock was so great, I couldn't wait to get home.'

She sighed loudly and rested her chin on her knees.

'Tell you what,' said Derek, determined to jolly her out of her mood. 'Why don't I go ashore with you and help you find somewhere to make that phone call? . . .'

One of the crew helped them untie the rowing boat, and they rowed across the shimmering water to the marina. In the distance there was a faint thumping from the discos of Marmaris.

After searching the narrow streets, which were thronging with promenaders and purveyors of coffee, sweetmeats, carpets and Lacoste imitations, they found a smart-ish international hotel where Heidi could use her credit card to secure a call to Leofred's home number in London. She gave Derek a subdued grin when she emerged, and consented to stroll back with her arm in his, to the quayside.

They rowed back in silence. Finally, as they approached the schooner, Derek said. 'So you'll be jumping ship then?'

'Yes?'

'And going . . . where? Somewhere different?'

'Oh, it'll be different all right.'

'With or without telephones?'

'Without, I should think.'

'Good . . . before we get back on the boat, there's just one thing I want to do . . .'

Heidi tensed, hoping he wasn't going to kiss her or anything awful like that.

But instead, Derek reached for her shoulder bag and emptied out its contents. 'Right,' he said briskly, 'You won't need this . . .'

He found her Aircall bleeper and with an impressive overarm, hurled it into the water. Seconds later, the small black message retriever followed it, with a loud 'plop'.

'And you'd be a lot better off without *this*, I reckon . . .'

'Oh no, not my Organofax! . . . oh . . .'

Heidi reached out to stop him, but she didn't try very hard. She leaned over the side of the boat and watched until the final glimpse of white paper was swallowed up by the Aegean.

Then, for the first time in months, she threw her head back and laughed out loud.

Joan Grimmins had done it again.

Leofred came into *Dick's* to talk to Jay, and he saw her there in the office at his desk. Saw her, but didn't recognise her.

She'd shed yet more weight, so that now she was 'bosomy' or 'voluptuous' rather than fat. Her charms were revealed by a rather classy-looking white linen shirt, and her hair had been softly permed, so that it fell over her shoulders in a rippling, tousled mane.

It was eery, Leofred thought, as he leaned against the door of the office, uncanny. Only that morning Jay had been making unflattering remarks about Joan, but it was as if the more he disparaged her, the more she blossomed.

She was on the phone to a prospective client. ' . . . Yes, my name's Joan Grimmins . . . you may as well ask for me; in effect I'm the manager..yes . . . you're welcome. Goodbye . . .'

Leofred's blood reached boiling point.

'Joan, I'd like a word . . .'

'Yes?' The burgundy lip-gloss on her large mouth glistened at him in a challenging fashion.

' . . . You're fired!'

Joan just laughed pleasantly. 'Don't be ridiculous! If you're going abroad to try and find your sister, then you'll need someone to run your sorry excuse for a business while you're away.'

'How d'you know I'm going after my sister? . . . You mean you listened in to the private conversation I just had with Jay?'

'That's right.'

'Right – you're still fired!'

Joan laughed again, this time with derision. 'You'll have to take it to an industrial tribunal, and you won't have a leg to stand on. How can you complain about me putting in extra hours and helping the business run efficiently?'

The gleaming burgundy lips challenged him again.

'Look Joan . . .' said Leofred quietly ' . . . forget all that. Just tell me what it is you want. From me. From this place.'

'Aha!' said Joan, and this time she was almost flirtatious. 'You'll see . . .'

Percy Grieves, bereaved brother of the late Alf Grieves, was disembarking from a number fourteen bus as it came to a stop in the Fulham Road.

They'd wondered why Alf was so late in bringing the van back, he and his wife, and then they'd had the awful news about the heart attack. During some sort of office party, from the sound of it, alone in the office with one of the secretaries.

Good old Alf, thought Percy. He always was a randy old bugger . . .

Lucky that they'd managed to track down the address of the fancy new night club, and lucky Percy kept a spare set of keys. He found the van without trouble, parked in the yard behind *Dick's* club. The road tax was out of date, and he noticed that the rear number plate had been nicked and one of the tyres was very bald. Never mind, he only had to get it home. He wasn't planning on using it after that.

Percy drove at a sedate thirty to Kingston-on-Thames. He parked the van neatly in the garage, closed the up-and-over door with a resounding clang, and padlocked it.

Six

'Well at least that bloody ugly van's been moved!' said Jay Cathcart, as he looked out of the window of *Dick's* a few days later.

He and Leofred and Lez had convened in something approaching a council of war, or the nearest thing to one that has the chief of staff munching on pistachios and flicking the shells into the bin.

'So what's the scam, Leof? . . .' asked Jay, sending a shell, with daring accuracy, past Lez's right ear. 'You had this cryptic phone call from Heidi saying that she was on a boat somewhere, and was trying to arrange a flight to Israel . . . why *Israel* for Christ's sake? Why not the Bahamas, or the Virgin Islands . . . or even Australia?'

At the mention of his beloved homeland, Lez drained his can of lager, crumpled it in his fist and belched loudly.

Taking this cue, Leofred said 'Ah . . . well, that's where Lez comes into it. You see, he claims to have discussed Israel with Heidi, and he thinks he was the one who gave her the idea of going there.'

''Sroight, mate!' said Lez, with another appreciative belch. 'Give us yer nuts, will you, sport?'

Jay tossed a handful of pistachios to Lez, who caught them in his mouth. 'Hey, I mean . . . I'm not sure I understand this. She could be anywhere in Israel—'

'Doubt it,' said Lez. 'She doesn't know the place, right? But I told her about the kibbutz I went to, where it was, the name and so on. Chances are she decides to show up there.'

Jay frowned. 'Not sure this is on my reality map . . . She could be cooling out at the King David Hotel in Jerusalem. Or diving in Eilat—'

'Sure, but the risk's got to be worth the price of a plane ticket hasn't it? To get back those bloody reckies you're so steamed about.'

'So it's old Leof to the rescue then? Are you all set? Ticket booked? Bag packed? . . .'

Leofred returned Jay's smile with more confidence than he felt. He was not one of life's natural travellers.

'Be sure and report back the minute you know anything.'

Leofred extended his hand, which Jay slapped with a flattened palm, raised, and then clenched in a quasi-masonic farewell.

'Break a leg,' he said.

'Get laid,' said Lez.

At that moment, Heidi Plunkett was sitting on a bus.

She tried to remember the last time she had been on a bus, but couldn't. She had certainly never been on a bus like *this* before. Forget reclining seats, hostess service and air-conditioning. The seats had all the suspension of snooker tables and the air-conditioning was an open window that let in hot, dry wind and dust from the burning, barren landscape.

The bus was trundling over the Golan Heights, which was a militarised zone, and every five minutes the bus driver would stop to pick up a group of hitching soldiers, as he was obliged to by law.

Heidi had never seen such men. They were like gods, tall and strong and sun-tanned, but with fine bone structure and silky hair that was associated with Europeans rather than Middle-Eastern races. They hung indolently from the aisle-straps, chewing gum, and smoking pungent smelling cigarettes. One of them stood so close to Heidi that his Uzi machine gun dug into her shoulder. She inched away, afraid it might go off. There were women soldiers too, with beautiful, haughty faces; holsters and grenades the only accessories they wore with their uniforms. Heidi started to feel naked with no armaments.

The bus pulled up in the middle of nowhere, and the bus-driver indicated that this was where she should get off. She stumbled, rather dazed, onto the roadside and watched the bus trundle away in a cloud of dust.

It was extraordinary that the driver had known this was it, because there was nothing there. Unless you counted a corrugated iron shack with a handwritten sign that said 'PEPSI –'FANTA – 7–UP.' No kibbutz in sight, just a narrow track leading off the main road and across the expanses of sand.

Heidi wrapped her jacket round her head, Lawrence of Arabia style, and started to walk down it, dragging her small suitcase. After the seven hour journey from Tel Aviv she was longing to empty her bladder, but didn't dare squat down beside the track. Just in case somebody saw her.

The track continued for well over a mile, and then, finally, there was a sign; small, discreet, understated.

'Kibbutz Kfar Hasava'.

Whatever Heidi had imagined, it wasn't this. She thought it would be like the entrance to a country club, with a lodge and gates, or possibly a reception area. She shouldered her suitcase again, feeling a little like Dorothy on the yellow brick road. Suddenly, after a few hundred yards, there was a water tower, then long, low concrete buildings and trees . . . splashes of colour from brilliant hibiscus and morning glory . . . and finally, green. Vast acres of lawn, stretching away to an escarpment with a sheer drop and breathtaking views.

And beyond that, desert.

The kibbutz had been founded by English speaking Zionists, so it had been a simple enough business for Heidi to telephone from Tel Aviv and offer her services as a volunteer. She had been told to report to a lady called Mrs Mader. After sticking her head round the door of various buildings, which turned out to be the laundry, the sick-bay and the toilet block, she found the lady in question; a middle-aged Jewish matron with greying hair, dressed in shapeless khaki shorts.

She greeted Heidi without fuss, as if she had just popped to the kibbutz from somewhere down the street, rather than London, via Izmir, Istanbul, Larnaka and Tel Aviv. Heidi was about to discover that this was a typical attitude amongst kibbutzniks. If crazy, spoilt young Westerners wanted to *shclep* half way around the world just for the privilege of experiencing physical labour for no wages . . . well, let them. So what if many of them were *goyim?*

'I'll take you down to the house where you're going to be sleeping,' said Mrs Mader, once Heidi had handed over her passport. 'You're going to be sharing with another English girl.'

There was no clue in Mrs Mader's voice as to whether this was a good or bad thing. She led Heidi and suitcase down a maze of paved paths that wound their way between the kibbutz buildings and the patches of springy green buffalo grass.

The 'house' turned out to be a cube of concrete with a door and a window. In the one room, there were two single beds pushed up against the wall, end to end, a chair and a table. A bare lightbulb dangled from the ceiling. Right on cue, a cockroach scuttled across the bare concrete floor and disappeared into the bathroom.

Mrs Mader didn't seem to think there was anything to apologise for. She introduced Heidi to Emma, her room-mate, and left.

Emma had the loud, strident and rather rude voice common amongst very rich girls. It was strange to hear it in this concrete box, and to see her bare, brown feet shod in an ingrained layer of dirt rather than a pair of low-heeled pumps with bows on the front that she would have purchased at a shoe shop in Sloane Square.

'Hi!' she barked. 'Emma Cosworth-Smith. That's your bed there. Clothes and stuff in the wardrobe. You haven't brought very much with you – good. We get kitted out, only wear our own clothes on Friday nights. Come on, dump your things and I'll take you up to the *machsan*.'

The 'machsan' turned out to be the clothes store where garments were distributed. Had Heidi imagined a cross between Henry Bendel and Harvey Nichols? Hardly, but she had at least envisaged something resembling a little English corner shop. Imagine her horror when the machsan turned out to be a corrugated iron shack with graffiti on the walls and no lighting, let alone changing rooms.

The nearest thing to this that Heidi had experienced was going to have her first school uniform bought for her at an old-fashioned outfitters. The motherly woman in charge clucked over her, holding up shirts against her back to get the right size. Finally she was handed what looked like a bundle of old rags: faded indigo coolie shirts and men's shorts, and a shapeless cotton pinny.

'But these aren't . . . I mean, somebody else has worn them.'

Emma brayed loudly. 'Of course. All the clothes are communal. You wear them, they go the the laundry, you pick up some different ones. I tell you, it's just as well we don't wear our own. Just wait and see how dirty they're going to get.'

'What – now?'

'Yah. You're working in the avocados. I've been told to take you up there as soon as you've changed.'

Heidi wondered if she knew about the seven hour bus journey preceded by a night flight. 'Perhaps, I'll just have a nap for a few hours—'

'Look—' said Emma, 'You're here to work, aren't you? If you try and skive off you won't be popular with anyone. They think the volunteers are lazy enough as it is.'

Heidi changed into her coolie clothes, tied a bandana round her head, and emerged quite camouflaged, except for her pale skin. Emma dragged her off to a waiting tractor, leapt onto it and flung it into gear as confidently as if it was a Golf GTI. Heidi clung on behind her as it bumped down a track and out into open countryside, past fields and orchards. Eventually they stopped in a plot of avocado trees. Dotted amongst the shiny green, were patches of now-familiar faded blue cotton, as a dozen workers pulled down the fruit.

'Go over and introduce yourself to Schaul – he's the leader of this group. I'd better get back to the bloody grapefruit. See you tonight . . .'

It wasn't difficult to work out which one was Schaul. The big one shouting at the others. He didn't take any notice of Heidi's arrival. She planted herself in front of him.

'I'm Heidi Plunkett.'

'So?' Schaul wore a grubby white vest, which did little to conceal the thick, black hair on his chest. And on his back and shoulders. Underneath, his skin was tanned to the colour of shoe polish. He had five days growth of black beard, which gleamed with fresh sweat. His eyes were very dark, and very bright. 'You here to pick avocados? If so, what are you waiting for? If not, get out of here. You're slowing things up.'

Heidi was unprepared for this charming speech of introduction. 'Where should I start?' she asked.

'I suppose you have a university degree, too? Where you see fruit on the trees, of course! My God, these volunteers! . . . And do up your shirt. I can see your tits!'

Schaul strode away. Cursing him under her breath, Heidi selected a tree and began to pick.

She had only harvested three avocados before she started to feel exhausted. She had picked fruit before, in Kent, but not in ninety degrees of mid-day heat. And the bloody things were so difficult to pull off the branches . . .

There was a shady patch underneath the tree, so Heidi leaned against the trunk and stretched out her legs. She wondered if there was any chance of a cold beer.

Schaul truly had eyes in the back of his head. He spotted her from fifty yards away and broke off the stream of Hebrew he was delivering to his workers to swear at her in fluent English. Schaul was a *sabra*, born in Israel, but his parents were first-generation English speakers, and he switched to and fro between the languages with astonishing speed.

'What the fuck are you doing? You'll be filing your nails next!'

Heidi was not one to be pushed around, but she was so hot and tired she had temporarily lost the ability to put up a fight. 'I needed a rest,' she said.

'A REST!' roared Schaul, his black eyes flashing fire. Drops of his sweat showered on Heidi's legs. 'Do you think we built this country out of rock and sand by taking rests? Do you think we wandered the earth for a thousand years and were slaughtered in our millions to let people like you take rests?'

Heidi hoped this was a rhetorical question.

'. . . this fruit that we're picking is our food! Don't you understand that? We don't have credit cards, and bank accounts here! We don't have money! We work to live! And we have to work without rest because we never know when we're going to have to stop to fight off the Syrians or the Lebanese!'

This speech made Heidi feel quite faint. In fact, she *was* going to faint. What a stroke of luck!

Schaul must have noticed her pallor, because he softened up. 'You can have five minutes, and a drink of water. Then, back to it.'

'Thanks.'

Schaul flashed her a smile. He squatted down and grubbed in the earth, picking up the sandy soil and dribbling down his face. 'This earth . . . this land . . . it means everything to us. And this fruit . . .'

He yanked an avocado from the tree, and with a savage movement of his teeth, ripped off the knobbly skin. The green flesh was crushed between his fingers.

Schaul looked down at the buttery slime as though he'd never seen it before.

'Will you sleep with me tonight?' he asked.

'I doubt it.'

'Pity. I find you quite sexy.'

When the telephone rang, Jay Cathcart was enjoying a back-rub from his wife.

'Get that, darling!' he ordered Saskia.

'Which phone?' she asked.

Jay motioned impatiently to the cordless and she handed it to him.

'Hi! Jay Cathcart speaking.'

'*It's Leofred.*'

'You've found out where they are! Great!'

'Actually, I was just ringing to say I've landed safely at Lod Airport and I'm taking the next bus up to the kibbutz.'

Jay evaded Saskia's ministering hands. 'Hey, give me a break, Leof! I told you to report news, not non-news!'

'Sorry.'

'Hey, I'm just uptight, that's all. We had the accountants in this afternoon, and the Club's making more of a loss than we anticipated. They're talking cash-inject city. And I haven't got Heidi here to russle up some dosh-spinning ventures, damn the flakey little . . . I've got to get a hit released, fast, or its curtains time.'

'Sorry.'

'We're all counting on you Leof . . . Leofred, are you there, man? You've gone all faint . . .'

'Did you have a fun time today? Do you think you're going to like it here?'

Emma Cosworth-Smith was addressing Heidi. They were amongst a group of volunteers sitting on the steps of one of the concrete cubes, in the dark. They were drinking Jack Daniels and listening to Bob Dylan singing 'Tender Loving Blues'.

'Yes, I do,' said Heidi, surprising herself. Despite the aching in her back and legs and the sunburn on her face – or perhaps because of them – she felt relaxed. The kibbutz was stranded in a strange sort of time warp. Heidi was too young to remember much about the hippy era, but she imagined there were similarities. She felt . . . hippyish, and she was rather enjoying it, For example, a male hand was stroking her bare leg, but she didn't care at all.

The 'high season' was over, and there were only about twenty volunteers left on the kibbutz. A handful of them were English; the rest were made up of Australians, South Africans, two Americans, one Dutch girl and one French. When Heidi had questioned them, she discovered that the common link was their reason for being there; all of them seemed to be running away from something. One of the boys, a Londoner called Sean, had fled from trouble with the police. One girl had a step-father who beat her up, another had lost her home and possessions in her divorce. Even Emma, the displaced Sloane, claimed she 'just *had* to get away from London'.

'I was getting in such a mess,' she confided to Heidi. 'I was in a *rarely* bad way.'

'What happened?' Heidi had asked, imagining the death of a close relative, a boyfriend.

'*So* many parties,' lamented Emma, as though she'd been forced to attend at knife-point. 'I could never get up on time in the morning, and I kept getting fired from my jobs. Daddy stopped my allowance when he found out I was doing drugs, and my overdraft was just *enormous* . . .'

Patti Smith was singing 'Frederick' now, and the EEC contingent was singing along. There was a rumbling noise in the darkness and a tractor drew up outside the house. Schaul was on it, and one of the kibbutz shepherds, a young *sabra* called Oran, who had woolly blond hair, greyed with dust, and a face like one of the animals he worked with.

Oran jumped down from the tractor, snatched the Jack Daniels bottle from an outstretched hand and sat down to drink it, without a word to anyone.

How rude, thought Heidi primly.

'Hey, you – Plunkett – up here!' shouted Schaul, patting the tractor seat.

'No thinks, I'm okay here . . .' began Heidi, but several pairs of strong hands grabbed her and handed her up to Schaul, amid much laughter. She was being kidnapped.

Schaul didn't laugh, he didn't appear to even look at her.

He just drove the tractor off into the dark, and turned down a bumpy track.

'Where are we going?' demanded Heidi, clinging on to his shirt so that she wasn't thrown off. She couldn't help noticing that he had a strong, clean smell. It must have been the soap flakes they used in the prehistoric kibbutz laundry.

'To the avocados, of course,' said Schaul, with a certain scorn.

They came to a halt in the orchard, and Schaul just sat there for a moment, his eyes glinting in the pitch blackness. 'I come up here every night, to make sure that everything's all right. And to say goodnight to them.'

He climbed down from the tractor and stood examining the patch of land that was illuminated in the headlights. A big, plump specimen sat there on the soil, waiting for him, presumably.

Schaul held it aloft. 'I love these avocados!' He clutched it to his bosom.

Heidi sat motionless on the tractor, displaced by a jarring sense of disbelief. Was she really sitting here in the dark, in the middle of a stony desert, with hostile Arabs only a few miles away, watching a large, hairy man hugging an avocado pear?

Schaul didn't seem to require any comment on this ritual, nor did he explain why Heidi's presence was necessary. She in turn, had already come to the conclusion that everyone in this place was mildly crazy, so didn't offer an opinion.

They drove back to the kibbutz in an unreal silence. Schaul stopped the tractor outside his own house, which was an older, moderately more sophisticated concrete cube with a small garden.

'Doesn't my date even drive me home?' asked Heidi.

She assumed he was going to ask her in, but then she

saw a shadowy figure sitting on the steps, waiting. One of the kibbutzniks, of the female variety.

'Oh, there's Ilana,' said Schaul, casually. 'I expect she wants to sleep with me tonight.'

Ilana didn't even look up.

'See you at work then, in . . .' Schaul looked at his watch. ' . . . about four hours time. And don't be late.'

Somewhat dazed, Heidi stumbled from the tractor and along the maze of paths until she reached her own house.

Or she *thought* it was her own house, but glancing through the mosquito screen door, she could see that there were already two people in there.

In the full glare of the naked light bulb, Miss Emma Cosworth-Smith was lying on her bed, entangled in the dusty brown limbs of Oran, the sheep man.

But he's not even attractive . . .

Despite herself, Heidi's prurient instincts overcame her and she stood staring at them, trying to work out which bit of body belonged to whom.

'Hi!' shouted Emma, 'Come in. There's plenty of room!' She pointed to the patch of Heidi's bed that they hadn't overflowed onto.

'Er, no thanks.' Heidi shouted back. Despite acting like a hippy, and despite the heady sense of unreality that takes over in cases of extreme exhaustion, she had no desire to share her bed with a man who looked and smelled like a sheep. She found a rug that someone had left outside that evening, and curled up on the step, counting avocados until she fell asleep.

Some six hours later, Paul Latchkey was already sitting at his desk in the Rapier Industries headquarters in London.

He was one of an elite group who had been summoned

in early that day, as they were being taken on a special outing. Like good little children going on a Sunday school picnic, they had to present themselves, clean and decent, in plenty of time before the charabanc arrived.

Paul was feeling anything but festive. In fact, he had never felt worse in all his life. There was a cold, slow burning in his stomach, like a combination of pre-dentist nerves and headmaster's study-itis.

He had done it, it was his fault. He would be single-handedly responsible for the ruination of a multi-million pound company.

There was tangible evidence on the desk in front of him. It took the form of *Research International;* a glossy trade magazine. The cover had a stagey, still-life close-up of a limp condom, a pink, rubbery diaphragm and a packet of pills.

'SEX IN THE '80s SURVEY!' shrieked the headline. *'Shock results inside.'*

Paul turned to the article that he had already read, line for line – even between the lines – several times.

'A major survey mounted exclusively by Research International has revealed a surprise crisis in Britain's contraceptive industry. The industry is reeling at evidence that their products are not being bought any more. Even with the concern over AIDS, the 25–45 age group are using fewer contraceptives than ever before. Our in-depth study has exposed a behavioural basis to this trend. The young people of '80s Britain have as their foremost concern the furtherance of their career. Quite simply: yuppies aren't having sex any more.'

There were two pages of the article, more findings and an impressive collection of statistics to back it all up.

Paul closed the magazine with a weighty sigh. He saw himself as a tragic, Shakespearian figure. Like so many others before him, he had been blinded by ambition. Now he was going to have to own up. There was nothing else for it.

The phone on his desk rang.

'Reception here . . . Mr Cathcart and his party are waiting to leave.'

Paul put the incriminating evidence into his briefcase and stumbled off to meet his fate.

Two hours later, he was in the wake of the great man himself, along with several other Rapier-ites, being given a guided tour of the company's pharmaceutical plant in Slough. As a special treat they had been flown there from London in a private light jet. There had even been champagne.

' . . . And this is where the tablets will be packaged,' boomed Ivo, waving his hands expansively over conveyor belts and sorting machines. ' . . . I think you'll agree that we did the right thing as far as presenting the product is concerned. We thought a conventional cardboard packet would be too "safe". So we went for these . . .' He held up a bright, shiny, pink plastic dispenser. ' . . . on the grounds that yuppies would like something a little more adventurous. Isn't that so, Paul?'

Like a teacher sniffing out his favourite pupil, Ivo located Paul Latchkey at the back of the group. He blushed and nodded, but the expression on his face was glum rather than proud, and he stared down at his briefcase rather than look Ivo in the eye.

Putting this down to modesty, Ivo led his favoured employees into the next warehouse. Here, the tablets were actually being made, cascading out of plastic chutes in their thousands, like large pink grains of sand.

Ivo strode over to one of the receiving bins and dug his

hands into it, sifting the pills with his hands. He lifted a few hundred of them up and let them trickle through his fingers with a thin, rattling sound.

'Beautiful sight, isn't it? The final product, at last. ZXT 45 . . . or Contracon, as we have to remember to call it now . . . these little darlings are going to revolutionise sex in this country. And we are the ones who are going to rake in the profits—'

There was a strangled sound behind him, something between a cough and a gasp. Ivo turned round and saw Paul's face, no longer pink with embarrassment but purple with agitation.

'Ivo . . . I . . . sorry to interrupt . . . but, I think this is important . . . I'm afraid . . .'

He handed Ivo the copy of *Research International* with a trembling hand.

There was absolute silence from the Rapier employees as their leader glanced at the cover of the magazine, then ran his eye over the article inside. The only sound was the clicking and spitting of the tablets as they rushed from their chutes.

'I need that chopper you had on stand-by,' said Ivo finally, addressing the factory manager. 'Now. And I need you.' He plucked young Paul out of the crowd, ' . . . because the two of us have got some talking to do.'

There was no talking in the helicopter. Ivo clamped the headphones on his head and looked straight ahead, while Paul, who had never been in a helicopter before and was disturbed by its angry, swirling motions, was sick into his briefcase.

When he finally removed his head from the region of his knees, the chopper had come to land on the roof of Rapier's headquarters and Ivo was already barking orders at his secretary. She was standing to attention on the roof, notebook in hand.

'Get Bob Wylde over to my office right away . . . and hold all my calls for at least an hour . . .'

It seemed several hours at least that Paul was in Ivo's office trying to explain his report on the market research findings. He waffled in a circular fashion about 'inconclusive evidence' and 'ambiguous consumer drift' until Ivo clicked his fingers with impatience and summoned Bob the chief accountant.

'What if,' he said to Bob without preamble. 'What if we call off the whole Contracon launch. Before we spend any more money on it.'

Bob shrugged. 'You should just about cover your losses by the next fiscal year.'

'And if we release the product and just hope for the best?'

'You risk putting an enormous hole in the company's resources if it bombs.'

'But that risk would be covered by a fully subscribed share offer?'

'A fully subscribed one, yes.'

Ivo tapped his pen rapidly against his desk. The tapping went on and on for what seemed an interminable time. Then he said, 'I'm going to do it. I'm going to believe in a product that the experts don't believe in. But to give people less time to change their minds, I want to bring forward the deadlines. Will you see to it, please, Bob?'

Bob wasn't happy. He took his own pen out of his pocket and started to chew on it.

'But Ivo, is this wise? The market's very volatile at the moment . . . and if we leave it as late as possible, wait for the dollar to stabilise, there's a greater chance things will settle down a bit—'

'No,' said Ivo. 'I've made up my mind. If the market's so volatile, all the more chance that rumours of a duff product will send down the value of our shares. I want those applications in by . . .'

He took his company calendar down from the wall and drew a big red ring around one of the dates.

' . . . Wednesday, 21st October.'

It was Friday, and on the kibbutz Kfar Hasava, Friday was the night to party.

Heidi was rather excited at this thought. At the end of her second day on the avocados she had either stopped feeling exhausted or she was so exhausted she felt exhilarated. She was starting to tan. And she had learned three Hebrew words – 'yes', 'no' and 'cucumber'.

On Friday evenings, all the kibbutzniks and all the volunteers gathered in the dining room for a ritual sabbath meal. The kibbutzniks were an irreligious lot, angering the local rabbis with their disregard for the marriage laws, and this meal was their token nod in the direction of Judaism.

'We get a bit dressed up,' explained Emma as she and Heidi showered off the filth of the fields. 'Look a little bit smarter than usual. I don't mean smart "smart" . . .' (Presumably smart "smart" was a little cocktail number you'd wear to a drinks party in the Boltons) ' . . . I mean kibbutz "smart".'

She proceeded to put on a pair of tennis shorts and a clean, if faded T-shirt. Heidi followed suit with a favourite vest and an old denim mini-skirt. She reached into the cupboard for her make-up bag.

'Stop!' cried Emma. 'No make-up!'

'No make-up?'

'No make-up.'

'Not even a bit of mascara?' pleaded Heidi, who was

desperate to detract attention from her sunburnt nose. 'No-one will notice.'

'They will!' said Emma. 'They notice everything about the volunteers, because we're the outsiders. And they disapprove of everything they notice. Especially make-up. The kibbutz women never wear any.'

'Why not?'

'They think it's tarty.'

'But they're so . . .' Heidi groped for the right word. Loose? Swinging? Easy?

Emma could offer no explanation as to why such a liberated people should frown so rigidly on Maybelline Fibre-free Waterproof Creme, so Heidi could only assume that it was a hangover from the judgmental wrath of their Old Testament god. She pondered the paradox as the two of them walked up to the dining room, where the Sabbath was about to be observed in a highly individual fashion.

Once everyone had gathered around the tables, the candles were lit and heads were hung, as one of the senior kibbutniks went through the prayers of blessing in a monotonous voice. Heidi had the distinct impression that he was hurrying them so that they could get on with the food. Sure enough, no sooner was the last 'amen' uttered than several brown hands shot out and grabbed the wine, rolls disappeared from plates and the religious observance was swallowed up in a noisy and drunken meal.

Once they had eaten their brown meat stew (mule, Heidi decided) and been served with coffee and cakes, the younger members of the community leapt to their feet and began to clear the tables and chairs with some impatience.

'Dancing,' said Emma. 'They always do it on Friday night.'

'Oh good.' Heidi was pleased. 'I feel like a bop.' She got to her feet with the others and started to flex her arms and legs in readiness for shaking them down to the hard, disco beat.

The music started on the prehistoric sound system . . . and Heidi quickly sat down again. The funky disco house rap was being played on mournful pipes and discordant fiddles. 'Bloody hell!' she said. 'Folk dancing!'

'*Riccadaim*,' Emma corrected her. 'Israeli dancing.'

Heidi watched in fascinated silence as the young kibbutz-niks, wearing expressions of the utmost seriousness, undu-lated around the room to the slow, haunting music. Their arms were held above their heads and their feet moved effortlessly in perfect time.

'Bloody hell,' repeated Heidi. Then: 'Can we join in?'

Emma laughed. 'You can try – look.'

Sure enough, some of the Australian volunteers were bumbling about on the floor, trying to copy the steps, but they looked like drunks trying to walk a straight line in comparison with the graceful Israelis.

After an hour or so of this humiliating display, once the volunteers had been put firmly in their inferior place, the lights were lowered and a few flashing coloured ones appeared out of nowhere. The folk music was ditched in favour of heavy rock.

'I can't dance to this!' sniffed Heidi, with all the snob-bishness of the hip Londoner. Then she remembered she was supposed to be acting like a hippy, so she got up and thrashed around wildly with everyone else. Very quickly she discovered that she was enjoying it much more than the dance floor at *Dick's* where one tried so hard to be cool that one looked as though one was retaining a coconut in one's rectum.

Dancing to early Doobie Brothers was sweaty work. Heidi couldn't help noticing Schaul, who was twisting his limbs as energetically as everyone else. Not only was he dressed in a clean white T-shirt and white jeans, but he had a white towel draped around his neck. She flailed her way up to him and tried to take the towel to wipe the sweat from her eyes.

But Schaul, of course, had other ideas. He looped the towel behind the back of her neck and used it to draw her close to him, pulling her after him as she danced, closer and closer until she could smell the soap amid the sweat, and the faintest, subtlest smell of avocados.

She closed her eyes, swaying seductively . . . but Schaul just laughed and danced away from her, waving his limbs faster and more wildly than ever with an astonishing energy. His white teeth shone blue in the ultraviolet light, and his white shirt and white jeans . . . all of him shining bluey white as she spun around the ring of dancers. Heidi felt small and silly all of a sudden, and went to sit down again.

The dancing went on until two, then gradually people began to disperse, in twos and threes and fours, some of them for more drinking, some of them for bed. Heidi walked alone down the crazy paving paths, heading for her concrete box.

Then suddenly he was there behind her, bounding down the path as though he was still dancing.

'There you are,' he said. 'Come on.'

They didn't talk on the way to Schaul's house, and when they got there, all he said was 'Coffee?' He moved about the room, lighting the gas ring, and the one lamp that cast a shadow up onto the bare wall. Heidi sat on the edge of the striped bedspread, waiting.

If he was going to seduce her, he was certainly in no hurry. He put a James Taylor record on an ancient turntable and sat sipping his coffee. 'I think I might go down and take a look at the avocados,' he said eventually.

But Heidi had come to a decision. 'Wait,' she said. 'Wait here a second, I've just got to go and fetch something.'

She ran out of the house and down the path to her own quarters, where she ignored the heaving of Emma and the sheep man and ran straight into the bathroom. Her hands shaking with nervous tension, she threw open the bathroom cabinet and started searching through it, knocking jars and packets all over the floor.

Finally she found them. The sample bottle that Ivo had brought home. ZXT 45.

She took out a pink pill and smiled at it. 'You,' she told it, 'Are about to revolutionise my sex life.'

She had forgotten how quickly the drug took effect. Even as she ran up the path to Schaul's house, she could feel herself beginning to salivate, and an alien heat running from her thighs to her groin and back again. By the time she flung open his door she was panting, and baring her teeth.

Schaul was fastening his sandals. 'The avocados' he reminded her.

'Bugger the avocados!' shrieked Heidi, crossing the room with one bound and silencing Schaul with a deafening shriek of lust . . .

At that moment the hapless Leofred was falling from a prehistoric bus and landing in a heap in the dust of the roadside.

Trying to spit the sand from his mouth as he walked, he followed the track to what he thought was its logical conclusion, and found himself in the middle of an Arab village. It took him a little while to work out that this was not the kibbutz (how was he to know the difference?) and to find out from the villagers where he had gone wrong.

When he arrived at the kibbutz it was three in the morning and it was very difficult to locate someone who was in charge. In fact it was very difficult to locate anyone, since it was pitch dark and all the buildings were locked.

Eventually, after walking in circles he found a group of people sitting on the edge of the swimming pool, drinking tequila from the bottle and singing 'The House of the Rising Sun'.

'Er . . . excuse me.' He squinted through the darkness 'Ah . . . does anyone know where I can find Heidi Plunkett?'

'Hang on, mate . . .' The voice was Australian. 'Did anyone see where Heidi went after the dancing?'

'Yeah. Come with me, and I'll take you.' This voice appeared to be South African. Leofred followed its owner through the darkness until they came to a small house, with a faint glow of light in the window. 'She'll be in there. See you later.'

Leofred pushed open the door and there was his sister. Naked. In the arms of a huge, swarthy Israeli.

He said the only thing that he could think of.

'Er, we were wondering where you put Sammi-Dawn's records . . .'

Seven

Two weeks later: Monday 19th October.

Leofred Plunkett was waking up and preparing himself for work.

He rolled off his narrow pallett, covered only with a single sheet, and sauntered into the bathroom, whistling 'Like a Rolling Stone'. The icy water from the shower was only bearable for a few seconds before he rushed out again, towelling himself furiously. Then into his faded blue shirt and shorts, already softened and primed with a layer of sweat and dirt. Leofred smiled. They felt good.

Outside the house, his fellow labourer, Gadi, was already waiting with a tractor and trailer.

'Morning, Gadi!' Leofred shouted, leaping into the trailer. Gadi responded with a brief nod and turned the tractor down a steep path. They stopped a few more times and picked up more workers – some volunteers, some kibbutzniks – who climbed into the trailer with Leofred.

Their destination was a large, empty area of waste land, on the edge of the escarpment overlooking a magnificent valley. That valley, Leofred had been told, was Syria. Which meant that they were now in the firing line. He tried not to think of that as he worked. They were turning this area of ground into a field, which would be irrigated and planted and turned miraculously green. But first they had to remove the stones from the ground, every single one, however small.

The women combed the soil for smaller fragments while Leofred and the other men grappled with the large rocks and heaved them over to the waiting trailer. It was back-breaking work, but to Leofred, wholly satisfying. As he straightened up in the sun to wipe the sweat from his face, he tried to remember what day it was, but found he couldn't. He couldn't even remember how long he had been here on the kibbutz.

He could remember the night of his arrival, however, and he laughed as he recalled how his one concern had been to place the vital phone call to Jay Cathcart. He had simply been unable to understand Heidi's *laissez faire* attitude.

'It's too late now.' she had told him from the arms of her lewd, hairy *sabra*. 'Do it tomorrow.'

'But tomorrow's Saturday.' Leofred had pleaded. 'I may not be able to get hold of him!'

'So? Then do it on Monday.'

By the time that Monday had arrived, Leofred's brain had been affected by excesses of alcohol, sun, and strenuous labour, and a lack of sleep. He felt light-headed and unwound, as though a piece of elastic inside him had been uncoiled and stretched to its logical limit. As he and Heidi had sat side by side in the kibbutz dining room, munching on sour cream and cinnamon pancakes, he had said to her, 'Oh yeah, I'm supposed to be phoning Jay, aren't I? I suppose I'd better do that this morning.'

He had made the call from an old 1930s style black telephone in the kibbutz office. It was the only one in the entire place, and used with a certain reluctance. Like make-up, telephones were disapproved of.

Leofred had had to rack what was left of his brain very hard to remember the number he was supposed to be ringing. Eventually he got through and there, suddenly, was Jay's familiar voice saying, '*Heyy! What's shaking, Leof?*'

Leofred had then given the answer which he knew would be completely unsatisfactory. 'She says the singles were in the van.'

Back in London, Leofred's phone call had prompted a crisis meeting.

'Go away.' Jay had said rudely to Joan Grimmins, who was in the office of *Dick's*. 'This is a crisis meeting.'

Joan was around so much these days, he kept on tripping over her. In fact, it was impossible for Jay to ignore the fact that she now looked genuinely . . . attractive. There was no other word for it, and even that was possibly an understatement. She had lost at least two stone since Leofred had first employed her, and her taste in clothes was becoming positively racy.

'You skirt's too short.' was all the criticism that Jay could dredge up on this occasion. He looked down at her legs. 'It's not suitable for work.'

One of the waitresses roller-skated by in a skirt that barely reached her crotch. Joan just smiled.

Gerry Gyles took charge of the crisis meeting, since Jay was having trouble controlling his frustration.

'They were in the sodding van!' he kept moaning over and over again. 'I don't believe it! They were in there all the time. Why didn't we look? . . .'

'The first thing you do in a crisis,' said Gerry, his medallions glinting on his luxuriant chest hair. 'Is get on the phone.' He brandished his own. 'Right, young Tim?'

'Right,' agreed Tim Goldsmith.

Gerry's fingers had long been in training for an occasion

such as this. With the astonishing speed of the professional telephone junkie, he worked his way through a series of numbers until he located the late Alf's next of kin, his brother Percy.

The others listened with rapt attention while Gerry asked the crucial question. Where was the van?

'You decided to sell it? . . . but until then you hadn't bothered to open it and look inside . . . the purchaser took a quick look inside and said he'd take the whole thing . . . said there was nothing but rubbish in there . . . so who did you sell the van to . . . a *scrap merchant?* . . .'

Gerry put the phone down. 'It's no good,' he said. 'We're too late. The whole lot's been scrapped. Sammi'll just have to re-record.'

'There's no time!' groaned Jay. 'I need the royalties. Like now.'

A glint had appeared in Gerry's eye. He was having another of his ideas. 'We could still re-record,' he said. 'And use ". . . Sexy" as a follow-up single later . . .'

'You don't mean? . . .'

'I do. We've still got "Nelly". It's gone straight into the charts in Italy. We could release it here.'

'No way,' said Jay emphatically. 'They'll never go for it. The DJ's will pan it to death.'

'It doesn't matter,' said Tim; eager to show off his knowledge of the 'biz'. 'The public could still make it a hit. Look at "Ernie". Look at "Two Little Boys.", "Rene and Renate" . . .'

'The Smurfs,' added Gerry.

'True,' agreed Jay.

'So we'll try it then? "Nelly the Elephant" for the UK charts.'

'Why not,' sighed Jay. 'We've got nothing to lose except the reputation of Rapier.'

*

'. . . the reputation of Rapier Industries has been to an extent dependent on the outcome of this share offer, and will now be in some doubt as the price of shares plummets in the City today.

'The asking price is 225 pence for each share. In the light of today's crash, it is unlikely that they have a market value of much more than half that. Only twenty-four hours ago, it was expected that there would be queues in the street on Wednesday morning, the deadline for the Rapier share deal. But now, all that is in doubt. Apart from a few postal applications which have already been sent off, it seems unlikely that the public will be interested in what is in effect, worthless stock. Asked if he felt it was too late to cancel the flotation, Mr Cathcart—'

Ivo waved the remote control at the television in his office, switching it off. It was October 19th and already the lunch-time news was calling it Black Monday. Wall Street and the City of London were experiencing the worst stock market crash since 1929.

Bob Wylde was in the office with Ivo, but after hearing the news bulletin he didn't dare speak to his boss. As he reached for his solid gold desk lighter and lit a cigar, Ivo's hand didn't betray the merest hint of tremor but his face, normally a lively pinkish red, was ashen.

'Contracon was due to arrive in the shops today, wasn't it?' he asked Bob eventually.

'That's right,' said Bob. He spoke in a hushed voice, as though in the presence of a corpse.

'And no-one's going to buy the bloody things, right?'

'Probably not.'

'And now we're not going to raise the money to pay for it?'

'It seems unlikely, unless the market turns around in the next three hours.'

Ivo walked over to the drinks cabinet and helped himself

to a generous slug of brandy. 'So things are just about as bad as they can get?'

'Well, I wouldn't . . . yes.'

Ivo was putting on his jacket. He reached in the pocket for a set of car keys and jingled them in Bob's face. 'Come on, we're going out!'

Bob didn't understand.

'I want to go and take a look. I've never seen a crash before, have you?'

The two men climbed into the front of Ivo's white Bentley Continental and it shot out of the underground garage with a squealing of brakes. Ivo rarely drove himself, and he tended to forget how.

The wheel arch clipped a concrete column, and Ivo yanked the wheel away into a magnificent skid.

'This is fun!' he declared to the nervous looking Bob. 'What do you reckon, Bob? Stick some music on the stereo, for God's sake! Something appropriate.'

With Rachmaninov's second piano concerto thundering through its tragic cadences, the Bentley shot down Kingsway, round the Aldwych and down to the Embankment, heading east.

'Check the windows!' shouted Ivo above the din. 'See if anyone's jumping out.'

They didn't spot any suicides, but saw several frantic brokers, running round in circles like stateless ants, some of them with calculators, desperately trying to calculate the likely size of their golden goodbyes. One ran up to his seven-series BMW and embraced it, kissing the windscreen and sobbing his farewell to the status symbol he would shortly lose.

'Oh God,' said Bob, pointing. 'Oh no, look!' The biggest crowd of all; brokers, pressmen and interested onlookers, was gathered outside the glass-panelled head office of Midwest, the clearing bank that was handling the Rapier share offer. Hung from the top of the twenty storey structure was an enormous banner with the Rapier share price in hundred feet high black letters.

'Oh God!' said Bob again. He looked out of the windows on either side. 'If you step on it, we might just be able to do a U-turn and get out of here before anyone spots you.'

'Certainly not,' said Ivo calmly. He leapt from the car, and with Rachmaninov pounding after him at twenty decibels, strode up to the banner. And then, in full public view with three camera crews recording the event, he ripped it down and trampled on it.

' . . . *half an hour ago, tycoon Ivo Cathcart arrived in person at the Midwest building on Cheapside and removed the price banner from its place of prominence. His appearance was as unexpected as his actions, and afterwards Mr Cathcart simply jumped into a waiting car and sped away without talking to newsmen. It is generally believed that the timing of the share offer this week, which was nothing more than sheer bad luck, could have a devastating effect on the Rapier Group of companies—*'

'Tune it in to Radio One!' shouted Gerry Gyles, 'They're about to do the chart run-down!'

He was in Jay Cathcart's office at the recording studios, and this time he had his protegée with him. Sammi-Dawn was sitting on the sofa, swinging one ripped denim leg and chomping on nuggets of Bubblee-Gumm, which Gerry supplied her with to stop her from yawning, rudely, in front of her benefactors. Every so often she would blow a large puce bubble in the direction of the ceiling.

Jay, Gerry and Tim were not interested in her behaviour today; in fact they hardly seemed to notice her at all. The three of them were huddled around the tuner in the compact stereo system, awaiting the fate of 'Nelly the Elephant.'

'. . . well, we're into the top five now, and this week there have been some changes, I can tell you! In fact, Britain has a new number one! . . .'

A ripple of excitement ran around the room. Sammi's bubble exploded on her nose, and she retrieved it delicately with her tongue.

'Get on with it, you old windbag!' Gerry urged the meandering DJ.

'. . . so there we have it, George Ridgeley at number five, with "Gimmee your sexy body". And at number four—'

('Number FOUR!' chimed the jingle)

'. . . number four is the Hat Shop Boys with "Anguish". In the number three slot—'

('Number THREE!')

'I don't think I can hack this build-up!' groaned Jay.

'. . . we have David Bauhaus with "Get Out of My Way". Which is an appropriate title because there are only two records standing between him and that chart-topping position. At number two—'

('Number TWO!')

'. . . is last week's number one, the St Enid's School Choir, singing "I love my Granny." And so, this week's number one—'

('Number ONE!')

'. . . knocking those St Enid's girls off the top slot, a record released two weeks ago, only entering the charts last week at number thirty seven—'

'It's got to be!' cried Gerry.

'. . . the surprise smash hit of the year, from a little lady who used to be a model and is now all set to be a top rock star . . . Britain's number one is Sammi-Dawn Thwort with her disco version of "Nelly the Elephant"!'

There followed general whoops of delight, and then cries of self-congratulation.

'Of course, I knew it would be a hit.' said Gerry.

'Me too,' said Tim, fetching a bottle of vintage Laurent Perrier from the fridge and handing it to Jay to open. 'I said so, didn't I?'

'What we need now,' mused Gerry as he sipped his champagne, 'Is to get her back on the front page of the papers . . . get you around town a bit more, eh Sammi?' He shouted over his shoulder without bothering to look round. 'I know . . . I've got it! We'll start a rumour that she's pregnant!'

'Brilliant!' said Tim.

' . . . we'll keep the father's identity a secret at first, get all the paper's inventing their own theories . . . this is the sort of thing the Sundays love . . . then we'll suggest it's someone famous . . . a top TV presenter—'

'Brilliant!'

' . . . Then of course the whole thing will be revealed as a hoax and she can go on all the chat shows and talk about her relationship with the press and the meeja in general . . .'

Jay was not joining in this happy speculation. He hung his head over his glass of champagne and looked gloomy.

'What's wrong, mate?' asked Gerry. 'We've got you your hit, haven't we?'

'The crash,' said Jay. 'I'm a much poorer man than I was yesterday. Most of my capital was in stocks and shares. In fact, we're talking disaster here.'

Gerry waved his hand airily, jangling his gold ID bracelets. 'Why worry? You still own a recording company that's about to mint it! We'll have the second version of ". . . Sexy" ready in a couple of weeks, won't we young Tim? And that'll be following "Nelly" up the charts—'

'Hey, you don't understand! I've got no assets left, my

billionaire brother – fount of all cash – is bankrupt, the girl who runs my nightclub legs it off to the Middle East, followed by her spaced-out brother who's supposed to be running my strippogram business . . . it's going to take more than a couple of disco hits to change *my* life around!'

Gerry put an avuncular hand on Jay's shoulder and poured him some champagne. 'Relax! We've got plans for a Christmas album, haven't we, Tim?'

'That's right.'

' . . . and I've had a sure-fire idea for the third single. I thought she could do a rap number. In fact, Tim got together with Miker Gee's producer and they came up with something specially for us. It's called the "Shopping Rap". Give Jay a burst, young Tim.'

Tim cleared his throat. 'Er, it goes . . .' He adopted a suitably unswerving monotone: *'Well-I've-been-to Chelsea-Fulham-Road-and-Knightsbridge-AND-I've-cleaned-out-Harvey-Nicks-Harrods-and-Miss-Selfridge . . .'*

'What d'you reckon?' asked Gerry. 'What do *you* think, Sammi love? . . . Sammi? . . . *Sammi!*' He turned round, but the sofa was empty. Sammi-Dawn had left the room without any of the others noticing.

'Where the hell's she got to?' stormed Gerry, 'Silly little—'

'Shall I go after her?' offered Tim.

'No, no, you're all right. I'd better go . . .'

Gerry walked out into the corridor and peered down the staircase. He thought she had probably gone to get herself a Pepsi, but there was no sign of her in the company cafeteria, or the front hall.

'Miss Thwort?' he asked the receptionist.

'She left.' The girl pointed to the front door.

'Oh shit!' Gerry darted out onto the street just in time to see the denim-clad figure disappearing down Warwick

Avenue. He pushed his sleeves up above his elbows, thrust his phone into his back pocket and ran.

Gerry hadn't run anywhere for at least fifteen years, and by the time he caught up with Sammi he was severely winded. She just gave him a pitying look and stuck out her arm to flag down an approaching double-decker.

'Sammi!' gasped Gerry. 'What do you think you're doing? We're discussing your career back there, your new single! You can't just—'

'Not going to make a new single,' Sammi popped a fresh Bubblee-Gumm in her mouth.

'But Sammi, in the rock business—'

'I don't wanna be a bleedin' rock star. I don't like it!'

The bus trundled to a stop and a group of passengers started to disembark, momentarily obscuring Sammi from view.

'But what about your future!' Gerry yelled over their heads. He resorted to a few of his best bribes. 'If you come back now and behave like a good girl, I'll take you down to St Tropez . . . I'll buy you a convertible . . . I'll introduce you to Jonathan Ross! . . .'

Sammi just sniffed and climbed onto the platform.

'Look, wherever you're going love, let me drive you in the Merc. You can't use public transport! . . . people will see you! . . . the paparazzi will photograph you! . . .'

But his pleas fell on deaf ears. Sammi-Dawn blew a large pink bubble in the direction of Gerry's face then disappeared out of sight on a number fifty-five bus to Plumstead Common.

At *Dick's*, Joan Grimmins was taking every available opportunity to build up the strippogram business.

'. . . We have a new attraction starting today.' she told

prospective customers. 'It's called a Crashogram. If you wanted something a bit topical, a bit humorous . . . What is it? . . . Well, a man dressed in a pin-stripe suit and bowler hat comes into the party with a noose round his neck. He fires a revolver at his head and then jumps out of the nearest window . . . you'd like to book one of those? . . . I thought you might . . .'

Joan spent the whole morning on the phone and took twenty Crashogram bookings. Then she put her mind to doing the accounts. Business had been doing very nicely since Leofred had gone away. Very nicely indeed . . .

After she had checked the petty cash till, Joan worked out the month's profits. She calculated how much of that sum belonged to Jay Cathcart, and typed it out as a formal statement. He would be surprised at the amount, she thought, and pleased too, no doubt. She put the statement into an envelope and wrote *'For the attention of Mr J. Cathcart'* with great care, in her best copperplate handwriting.

'Fiddling the books, eh, darling?'

Lez had come into the office, fully dressed for once, and carrying a rucksack.

'Oi say, this crash business is a bit of a lark, eh? All those greedy bastards getting their come-uppance? What d'you reckon? Believe in retribution?'

Joan looked pointedly at the rucksack. 'Going somewhere?'

'Yeeh. The way things are going around here I reckon there won't be a job for me much longer, so I'm shooting through. Wondered if you'd like to come down the road for a farewell drink?'

'Why not?' asked Joan coolly. She shrugged on a very chic leather jacket and let Lez escort her down the Fulham Road as far as the Goat and Braces.

'You know,' said Lez, as they settled themselves at a

table with six pints of lager and a dry sherry. 'It's a ruddy shame you and me never had time to get together. It's only just occurred to me recently, but you really are a stunning sheila.'

Joan said nothing, just smoothing her rippling brunette mane.

'Still, they say it's never too late. How about it, a quickie? Love in the afternoon and all that . . .'

He manoeuvred a huge brown paw onto one of Joan's still-generous breasts. She pushed it away and continued to sip her sherry.

'Aw, come on! You haven't exactly been getting a lot lately. Reckon you must be pretty desperate.'

Joan's slickly coloured red lips parted in a smile.

'You're up to something, aren't you? . . .'

Another smile.

' . . . I thought as much. Going to tell me who he is?'

Joan gave one of her mirthless half-laughs.

'Reckon you don't need to tell old Lez anything. I see everything in that place — except when I'm in the dunny . . . I've seen the way you look at him, when you think he's not looking at you . . . well, you've got no chance, ya hear me? . . . No ruddy chance at all!'

The next morning found the intrepid Plunketts on a bus trip.

'Bus' was probably too elevated a word for what was essentially an open-sided truck, of the sort that sheep or cattle might travel in. Heidi and Leofred, along with about twenty of their fellow labourers, were going on a *tiul*; an organised day trip as a reward for their labours.

The radio in the cab was playing some wailing Arab hit as the truck bounced across an unsurfaced track. Heidi put on her Ray-Bans to keep the warm, sandy wind out of her eyes as she gazed across the desert landscape. Around her, the voices of the other volunteers were raised in philosophical debate.

' . . . I've always gone along with the theory that death is the ultimate orgasm. Personally.'

' . . . Nah, all that stuff's a con. Death's the end – lights out time.'

' . . . You don't know that. There might be a heaven, so why not believe in it? You just have to make the act of faith—'

' . . . Exactly: like gambling. And we all know gamblers never come out on top.'

' . . . You know what I think? Life is suffering. Death is suffering. So why not just get smashed? . . .'

This last comment was made with an Australian accent.

Heidi found her gaze coming to rest on Schaul. His elbows were resting on his hairy knees, and he was picking the soil from under his fingernails. When his eyes met Heidi's they betrayed only the merest flicker of recognition before he resumed his task.

After three hours the bus reached the coast, at a place called Achzif. By the standards of northern Israel it was a resort, which meant that it had a few sunshades made from palm leaves and some cold water showers that looked like watering cans.

Nevertheless, the holiday spirit was very much in evidence and Heidi was soon amongst all the others who were racing into the surf. The Australians rugby-tackled each other and tried to pull off the girls' bikinis; a job that had already been done by the waves in most cases. Even the taciturn Oran joined in the fun and games, after a fashion. He picked up Emma, carried her to the water's edge and ducked her under a wave.

Later, when Heidi was lying under a palm shelter and

munching blissfully on a choc-ice (sweet foods came in the same category as make-up and telephones), she opened her eyes to find Schaul beside her.

This was a most unusual turn of events. Normally he never spoke to her in public. Even when they were working alongside one another in the avocado fields he only ever said 'You've forgotten that tree' or 'Pick the big ones first'. He treated her exactly as he treated any other female volunteer, with tolerant contempt; the exception in her case being that after dark she came to his house and bounced around on his hard bed for hours on end.

'I think your brother's having a good time, today,' commented Schaul.

Heidi sat up and looked across to the sea, where Leofred was joining in a childish game of pebble throwing.

'Yes, he is. He really loves it here in Israel. I don't think I've ever seen him so relaxed.'

Schaul frowned, puzzled. 'So why doesn't he enjoy himself then? Why is he alone?'

'He's not alone, look! He's having some sort of a competition with Gadi . . . he and Gadi are great mates . . .'

Heidi's voice ground to a halt as she realised what Schaul had meant. He meant why didn't Leofred have a sex life, why did he sleep alone? That was most definitely abnormal in Schaul's eyes.

'Leofred's always been very shy with women, that's all. Maybe you could help him out? Fix him up . . .'

'It isn't necessary. Look . . .'

He pointed to the horizon. Leofred was being chased out of the surf and onto the beach by big, lusty Ilana.

' . . . I don't think he needs any help.'

*

As Leofred splashed out of the sea and headed for dry land, he felt the earth move.

One moment he had been looking up into a brilliantly blue sky; the next his body tilted through one hundred and eighty degrees and he was lying prone, with sand up his nose. He had felt the sensation of being winded from behind by some heavy, fast-moving beast like a Doberman dog.

He looked up into the shining white teeth and slavering jaw of Ilana, the kibbutz valkyrie. She was a tall, strong-shouldered girl with heavy thighs and a fearsome clump of black hair in each armpit. Leofred was more than a little afraid of her.

'Um . . . hi!' he said, digging his feet into the sand and pulling himself to his feet. He made as if to stroll up the beach in a casual fashion, but no sooner had he turned his back than a pair of hands went round his waist and tugged off his swimming trunks. Completely.

'Ah . . . d'you think I could have those back, please . . .'

Ilana held her trophy aloft, and it was impossible for Leofred to reach up and grab them and to keep his hands in a protective position over his private parts.

'Here, you can have them – catch!' Ilana flung the shorts up into the air, and Leofred was forced to expose himself if he was to stand any chance of retrieving them. Ilana stared, but not at his naked loins, as he might have expected. She was looking at his face with a puzzled air, as if she could not fathom his reaction.

'You are embarrassed?' she asked.

'Well, um . . .'

'Why? Don't you like bodies in England? Don't you enjoy them?'

'Well, we do . . . well, no, I suppose not. It's different there. Life is different.'

'Different better . . . or different worse?' demanded Ilana, legs planted astride on the sand, hands on hips.

'Better I suppose . . . I mean, we like it.' He pushed the image of Joan Grimmins from his mind.

'Why do you stay here, then?'

But Leofred had no answer for that, or if he did he had no intention of trying to explain it to Ilana.

Nevertheless she stuck doggedly at his side all day. Leofred lay on his towel pretending to sunbathe, but whenever he opened his eyes, he could see Ilana's big white teeth, glinting in the sun.

On their return to the kibbutz, the day's leave was rounded off by a special outdoor film show. There were not enough free chairs, so blankets and mattresses were dragged outside and arranged in companionable rows on the parched lawn.

As the flickering, grainy credits of *Return of the Pink Panther* (with Hebrew subtitles) rolled, and all was silent except for the bronchial hum of the projector, Leofred was not all together surprised to find Ilana lying two feet away from him. By the time Peter Sellers and Herbert Lom had done their first big scene, the two feet had diminished to eighteen inches. Then twelve . . .

As the action reached Gstaad, Ilana somehow contrived to be underneath the same blanket. For a while Leofred did the English thing and pretended it hadn't happened. He knew, though, that subtlety was not Ilana's strong suit, and soon she was going to do something to draw attention to her presence. They were both wearing shorts, and he could feel the thick, dark hair on her calves tickling his skin . . .

'Um . . . I think I'll go and get a drink of water. Back in a minute . . .'

Leofred managed to stay away for thirty-six minutes, by which time the film was over and the crowd seeking entertainment had moved on to singing songs round a campfire. Feeling guilty, he found Ilana and made a point of sitting next to her.

'Good film,' he commented. 'Funny.'

She didn't reply, and one look at her dark, brooding face in the firelight confirmed that she was sulking.

'Ilana, have I done something wrong?'

'You're a pig. An English pig.'

'Look Ilana, I do . . . I don't . . . I mean, I *do* find you attractive, very attractive, it's just—'

'You should go back to England if they are so wonderful there. You should go home.'

Sitting next to Schaul by the camp-fire, Heidi felt deeply content. He might not speak to her, or acknowledge her, but it was Heidi he wanted in his bed every night, and here that was as committed as you got.

Leofred didn't seem to be having much luck, though. Despite the heat of the fire, there was a distinct frost coming from Ilana's vicinity. Schaul had been wrong about that – he did need some help. And Heidi wanted to help him. In her benevolent glow, she wanted her brother to enjoy kibbutz life to the full.

He looked relieved when Heidi stood up and beckoned to Ilana to follow. He probably imagined his sister was going to dole out some girl-talk to warn her off. The thought made Heidi smile to herself as she led Ilana back to her house. But the girl-talk she had in mind was quite different.

'Here—' she said to Ilana. 'This is what you need.'

She held out a pink tablet.

'I'll show you how to use it . . . I can assure you it never fail—'

But Ilana was out of the house, the bit – so to speak – between her teeth. Not wishing to miss the fun, Heidi followed her up the path and was just in time to hear the primaeval snarl, and see Leofred disappear, legs akimbo, into a bush.

Three hours later, the bonfire had burned low, and the revellers had all but exhausted their repertoire of songs.

'You think of one, Heidi,' someone said, after they had sung 'Waltzing Matilda' for the fourth time.

'No, it's all right . . . I think I'll just go and stretch my legs.'

She was, of course, going to Schaul's house, and everyone knew she was going to Schaul's house, but some remaining trace of convention prevented her from just saying 'Oh, I think I'll go and see Schaul now.' Because they all knew what she and Schaul would be doing.

The light glowed from his window, as usual, and she walked in without knocking, as usual.

And found Schaul in bed with Dani, one of the more nubile teenage kibbutzniks.

'Oh . . . sorry,' was all she could think of to say.

Schaul gave her a small wave, over Dani's back, to indicate that it was okay.

Standing on the path, recipient of a sexual slap in the face, Heidi did not feel that it was okay at all.

'Okay?' called Rod, one of the South African volunteers, as he strolled past, no doubt on his way to some fevered nocturnal assignation.

'Er . . . yes, sure.'

Rod waited for her, so she walked beside him for a while. He was one of the longest-standing members of the volunteer community, a young Durbanite who had fled to escape his country's national service draft.

'Uh . . . Dani was in there.' she explained at last.

'Oh, yeah, Dani.'

'I thought she went with Gadi.'

'She did – after Ilana dropped Gadi to go with Schaul.'

'But Schaul dropped Ilana . . . and now she's with my brother.'

'Oh . . . I guess so.'

They walked on a little further, until they almost tripped over two bodies, writhing around on the grass, their legs blocking the pathway. The girl's face was obscured, but Heidi recognised the frenzied, ZXT 45-induced grunts. It was Ilana, with Emma's-ex, Oran the sheepman. So where was Emma?

Rod walked Heidi back to her house, and the question was answered. The light was on.

'Hi, Emma.'

Heidi walked in and found her room-mate naked on the bed, smoking an Israeli menthol cigarette to keep away the mosquitos. The closet door opened. And out walked Leofred.

Or rather he stumbled. Whatever Ilana had done to him, he could no longer walk.

'Oh God!' said Heidi. 'Not you two as well!'

'It's not what you think!' pleaded Leofred. 'I'm just trying to hide from Ilana!'

Heidi went and sat on the step next to Rod. She closed her eyes and let out a huge sigh.

'I know what you're feeling,' said Rod sagely. 'The merry-go-round effect. It gets to you after a while. People change partners like clothes. Nothing stays the same here for long.'

Heidi sighed again. 'Just when I was beginning to feel I knew where I was. Now I've got to get up in the morning and start all over again.'

'Hey, listen, this isn't the place for sexual fidelity. If you're feeling like that, maybe it's time you thought about going home?'

'But I love it here,' Heidi sounded miserable. 'And I don't want that old life in London.' She added fiercely: 'So materialistic, so shallow. This is still better.'

'But everyone has to go back some time. This is the way to look at it – that you'll be using the things you've learned here to change your life at home. For the better.'

'No,' repeated Heidi. 'You don't understand. I can't ever go back. Not ever.'

Eight

Two weeks later, Ivo Cathcart was spending his last morning at the head office of Rapier Industries.

Bob Wylde sat in the 'interviewee's' chair and watched as his boss tipped his executive desk toys into a waiting cardboard box. They were followed by a calendar, a heavy onyx lighter and lastly, a photograph of Heidi Plunkett. Ivo gazed at the photograph regretfully before he consigned it to the box.

'This isn't necessary, Ivo.' insisted Bob. 'Things really aren't so bad. We've got the final accounts in now, and they show that if you sell off some of the subsidiary companies – the Star Group, for example – you'll be able to start all over again on a slightly smaller scale . . .'

'Start all over again, eh?' Ivo started to stack files on his desk.

'Of course you could! The supermarkets and cinemas are all intact. And the name of Rapier still carries weight—'

'Rapier's finished – over.' Ivo made his point by ripping a pile of stiff, crested invitations in half. 'I want you to sell off everything for cash, and after all the debts have been settled and all the staff given severance pay, I want you to put whatever's left in the hands of my brokers . . . my stockbrokers.' He grinned at this irony.

Bob looked genuinely disappointed. 'Well, I must say, Ivo, it's not like you to give up. Not like you at all.'

Ivo turned back to his cardboard boxes without further comment. He couldn't even begin to explain. That he had simply had enough of being a tycoon. He was drained, resourceless. Being an industrial whizz-kid was like playing a complicated and dangerous board game. He had to be five steps ahead of the other players all the time and it had burned him out. And he was still several years short of his fortieth birthday.

'If that's all, Bob . . . I have an appointment.'

Since he had dispensed with his chauffeur's services that morning, Ivo collected the Bentley from the underground garage and drove himself out of London, down the A3 to Hampshire.

His destination was a rather fine country house – *his* house. He used to live there before his divorce from his first wife, Linda, and he still owned it, although he hadn't been there for over a year. The Bentley slid up the long drive, past the late-blooming roses and hydrangeas, and braked rather suddenly outside the entrance porch.

A man was waiting for him on the steps, clipboard at half-mast in a deferential manner. Mr Blade, of Blade Gaskett Hillsop the estate agents.

'Mr Cathcart . . . a pleasure . . . an honour. How may Blade Gaskett Hillsop be of service to you, Mr Cathcart.'

'I want to get rid of it.'

'Get rid of it? . . . You mean you want to sell? . . . You want to sell this spacious and desirable gentleman's residence with every modern amenity plus fine views and extensive grounds affording easy access to London?'

'Precisely.'

'Well, let's see now . . . it's certainly an A grade property, which means we would do a full colour brochure, high gloss, with photographs – front elevation, some interior shots—'

'How much will I get for it?'

'Ah, well . . .' Mr Blade walked around in a small circle and pretended to be examining an unusual feature of the brickwork. 'In terms of value, well obviously a fine property like this is beyond price, quite unique of course . . . about a hundred and fifty.'

'Thousand? Is that all? But I paid a quarter of a million for it seven years ago! It should be worth six figures! This is Hampshire, damn it, prime commuting territory!'

'Ah well, that's the point, Mr Cathcart, that is the point!' Mr Blade was in his professional element now. 'It's the stock market crash, you see. In the last few weeks, property prices have just plummeted. Plummeted! Between you and me, you'd be lucky to get rid of this for a hundred and fifty.'

'But that's ridiculous! This is the most prosperous corner of Britain!'

'Precisely!' Mr Blade tapped his clipboard for emphasis. 'This is the stockbroker belt, after all. Who but a stockbroker could afford a house like this? . . . With the exception of your eminent self, naturally . . . and where are all the stockbrokers and their money now?' He drew one finger across his throat and made a strangled sound. 'However, perhaps if you were to hold out for a foreign buyer, or—'

'Forget it.' said Ivo. 'I'll keep it.'

He had already turned his back on Mr Blade and was strolling across the lawn at the rear of the house. The gardener, Crouch, had just been spotted pruning a privet.

'Hey Crouch! Crouch . . . here a minute!'

Crouch was pale with shock. Not only had Mr Cathcart taken the unprecedented step of visiting his own house, but now he was about to speak to one of the staff too.

'I'd like you to dig up the tennis court, Crouch.'

'Beg your pardon, sir?'

'The tennis court! Dig it up! Leave that poxy hedge and make a start on it now . . . oh, and when you've finished, Crouch, I'd like you to fill in the swimming pool.'

'The swimming pool, sir?'

'That's right! Well, come on man, chop, chop! No time to waste . . .'

Having made a positive decision, Ivo felt all his old energy returning. He stripped off his Armani jacket and strode towards the tool-shed.

Crouch's mouth fell open as he stared, bewitched, at Ivo's embroidered, multi-coloured braces.

'Get on with it man, get on with it!' Ivo barked impatiently.

He disappeared into the shed and rummaged around in the dark until he found a hoe, or at least, what he imagined was a hoe. It might have been a pick. But that didn't matter. It was a tool – not a pen, or a calculator, or a telephone, but an honest-to-God tool.

He carried the hoe onto the immaculate lawn and found the symbolic centre point. Then, with a grunt of satisfaction, he made his first, attacking swing, and started to turn over the earth.

Sammi-Dawn Thwort was at home with her family in 32, Ingledew Road, Plumstead.

At last she was a part again of that tranquil domestic scene that she had missed so much. Her grandmother was watching an Australian soap opera with the volume turned up full, while her mother Doreen – now retired from her job as Drummond Industries' tea-lady – was munching a pound of Edinburgh rock and explaining the plot.

Her father, Ronnie Thwort, breeder of champion

Rottweilers, was house-training his latest litter of puppies, cheering them on as they ripped down the lounge curtains with their newly discovered teeth. Brother Daylon was in the kitchen, getting to grips with a Home-Tattooing Kit. Every so often, the booming Australian accents would be drowned out by howls of pain and the smell of singeing flesh.

'Wotchou got there love?' Doreen asked her daughter, craning her neck to look at Sammi.

'Me savings.' Sammi was sitting in the armchair, counting her way through assorted piles of cheques and fifty pound notes.

' . . . Ronnie, get them bleedin' animals off my best dralon! . . . let's have a look, love.' Doreen left her seat and shuffled across the carpet to where her daughter was sitting.

'Blimey, what a lot of money you got, gel!'

'From my modellin' jobs.' Sammi only glanced up from her counting to ask: 'What's that awful honk, Mum?'

Doreen looked down at her slipper. 'I must have trodden in something . . . oh no, not again! Not another one! GET THOSE DOGS BACK IN THEIR KENNELS RON THWORT, OR I'LL DROWN THEM! . . . so, wotchou going to do with all that money then, girl your age? Mind you, you'll need your savings, now you've packed in that singing business. Jobs aren't easy to find, not round here, and you've only got the two C.S.E.s . . .'

Sammi had stuffed the envelope of money into her clutch bag, and was putting on her best fun-fur. 'I'm taking it down the building society.'

'Well on your way back, love, will you stop off at Marine Fresh and get in some chips for our—'

But Sammi had already gone. Her stiletto heels made little scraping noises on the pavement as she tottered down the pavement to the High Street.

Her first stop was the estate agent, but she didn't go

in. She just gazed at the revolving felt pillars with the photographs pinned on them. She waited patiently, and finally the one she was waiting for slid into view. It was just what she had always wanted, and now that prices had fallen, nice and cheap. On a modern estate in Dulwich, a three bedroomed detached. With a sun porch.

She stomped into the Mutual Friendly Building Society and flung her envelope down on the desk as a challenge. 'I want to buy a house,' she told the girl assistant.

'I see. And you'd like us to help you with a mortgage? . . . Do you have any deposit at all?'

'That's it,' said Sammi, pointing to the envelope. 'Eleven thousand.' She popped a Bubblee-Gumm into her mouth and began to chew, quickly.

'Well that's a very good start, certainly. And how much would you like to borrow.'

'We want about forty grand.'

'We? Your husband? . . .'

'Me and Barry. M'boyfriend. Well, we're engaged.'

'And do you have jobs?'

'Barry's a messenger. On a bike. And I'm just on my way to get a job. Now.'

'Fine . . .' The girl ushered her towards the door. 'Well, when you've got the job sorted out, come back and we'll go through the figures.'

Sammi stood on the High Street and took stock. She'd never had what one might term a 'proper job' and her ideas about how you got one were a little hazy. Daylon was always talking about going down the Job Centre. That was probably the best place to start.

There was a row of little cards in the Job Centre window. Sammi pressed her nose against the glass and read them. Most of them seemed to be for men; fitters and mechanics . . . Ah, here was one for a girl.

'*GIRL WANTED: Everglade Home, Rawlinson Road.* 30

hours per week as auxiliary helper. Applicants must be patient, cheerful and unselfish, and love chatting to old people . . . '

Sammi sniffed, shouldered her fun-fur and set off for Rawlinson Road.

'It was the most happening club in town,' said Jay Cathcart sadly, 'For about two weeks.'

He and Andy the barman were clearing out *Dick's* club, packing up the 'effects' that the property management insisted were emptied from the place before it was let. In the office, Joan Grimmins was sorting out all the paper work, calculating final figures, making up pay packets. There was no sign of Saskia. She had not been seen at Jay's side for several weeks.

'Are you sure about this, Jay?' asked Andy, as he wrapped glitter-sprayed martini glasses in tissue paper. 'I mean, the situation might improve . . .'

'I'm sure, man, I'm sure.' Jay picked up one of the club's silver match books and sighed as he looked at the *Dick's* logo. 'I've lost my front of house manager, then my strippogram manager, then my bouncer. I've no longer got a hit-making rock star on the books, Gyles has run off somewhere with the European royalties from "Nelly" and my marriage is feeling the strain . . . Sas. has gone off on some modelling assignment in N.Y. . . .'

'Bad news all round then?' Andy started to empty the bottles of lemon vodka from the freezer.

'Bad news city. I don't know what I would have done without old Joan there . . .' Jay nodded in the direction of the office. 'She's made me a nice little profit on the strippograms, so I'll have some cash to put into my next business venture.'

Andy raised his eyebrows. 'Any idea what that will be?'

'Hey, this time I'm just aiming to go with the flow! See what's occurring out there on the street . . . get the buzz..'

'Anything to bring in a fast buck, then.' said Andy.

'Got it in one.' Jay managed a smile. 'Are you through there? . . . All packed up? So how about you and me cruising down to the Goat and Braces for a swift one?'

'There's plenty of drink here,' said Andy, pointing to a crate of champagne.'

'I know, but I just need to get out of this place. All this failure is driving me tonto . . .' He picked up a large handwritten sign and tucked it under his arm. 'And on our way, we can stick up this thing.'

He went out of the club, with Andy at his heels, and the two of them took the lift down to the ground floor. The sign was then attached with sellotape to the main door of the building . . .

'DICK'S CLUB CLOSED DUE TO FINANCIAL HARDSHIP.'

Joan Grimmins, looking out of the window of the club, watched Jay and Andy walk down the Fulham Road.

Then she went into the Ladies and examined her appearance in the mirror above the washbasins. Her hair frothed over her shoulders in Medusa-like waves, glinting with chestnut and amber low-lights. Her eyes, with their kohled rims and three layers of mascara, were sultry and mysterious. Morello-cherry lipstick gleamed on her mouth.

Joan adjusted the neckline of her dress, a skin-tight black lycra mini revealing every curve. It showed almost all of her legs, clad in sheer black stockings and patent leather stilettos.

She smoothed the dress down over her hips, and as she did so, she smiled. Her reflection smiled back at her. But this time it was not the usual joyless twisting of her mouth; this time it was a genuine, uninhibited smile of pleasure.

Because at last Joan had got what she wanted.

At that moment, an El Al flight from Tel Aviv was landing at Heathrow's Terminal Three.

Emerging from the plane, suntanned and fit, at least one of the passengers was having regrets about leaving Israel for England on a raw November day.

Leofred Plunkett elected to take the underground into the centre of the city. He could take the Piccadilly Line straight to South Kensington and then walk to the couple of hundred yards to the Fulham Road. When he had left England a month ago he had only intended to be gone a few days, so he didn't have much luggage with him.

He was hardly expecting a hero's welcome, but the sign on the door of the club still came as a shock. 'CLOSED DUE TO FINANCIAL HARDSHIP'. What did that mean?

He rang the bell repeatedly, but there was no answer. Turning to walk back to the tube station he did not see Joan Grimmin's face in the window, looking down, smiling.

Leofred's flat in Royal Oak was icy cold and full of dust. Just setting foot inside the place made him feel depressed. He switched on the central heating boiler and sat down on his bed, still in his coat, waiting for it to come on.

The phone rang.

'*Isn't it time you got an answering machine, you stupid dog blob!*' screeched the familiar voice.

Sandra.

'Oh . . . um, yes. I suppose I ought to . . .' Hearing Sandra's voice made Leofred feel vague, and tired. 'How are you, anyway?'

'Me? I've been going crazy trying to get hold of you! I've been phoning you for weeks! Where've you been?'

'Er . . . away. On business.'

'I wanted to know what you'd been doing with yourself since you got the boot from Drummond.'

'Well, not very much . . . that is, I *was*, but I'm probably not—'

'Good, 'cos I've got a proposition I want to put to you . . . not that sort of proposition, you dirty-minded little bugger . . .' Sandra sniggered. 'Strictly business. You interested?'

'Yes, of course.'

'Right. Get off your bum then, and meet me in the Italian caff at the end of your road. In half an hour.'

Leofred left his luggage where he'd dumped it in the hallway and went straight out, glad of an excuse to leave the flat. He sat at a corner table in the café, drinking endless cups of espresso and waiting for Sandra to arrive.

She bustled in, gold bracelets jangling, her huge earrings making indents in his cheeks as she kissed him soundly. She was now visibly pregnant beneath her flashy silk dress, and blooming.

'You look well,' observed Leofred shyly.

'Oh, I feel it, I feel it!' Sandra assured him. 'In fact, that's what this is all about. I've been feeling so well that I've got bored just sitting around on my arse all day, knitting bootees. So me and Julian have decided to go into business together.'

'Oh – that's nice.' Leofred still felt uncomfortable about his earlier judgement of Julian's sexuality.

Sandra's face had taken on a dreamy look, so he concluded she was probably still infatuated with the father of her unborn child. ('TOY-BOY DAD', the *Meteor* had called him when Sandra resigned) 'I'd put by quite a bit of cash when I was chairman, and we've found this lovely little restaurant in Richmond. It's right by the river – really pretty – and we're going to do traditional English with some French and Italian.'

'Super.' said Leofred.

'So how about it, then?' asked Sandra with a suggestive smile.

'Ah, well . . . I don't think . . .' Leofred found himself blushing.

'Not *that*, you stupid plonker! Christ, you always were a bit slow to twig. I mean how about working at our restaurant? We'd bring you in as an equal partner.'

'I'd love to,' said Leofred. 'In fact, to be honest Sandra, you've saved my life. I've just got back and found that my job seems to have, er . . . disappeared.'

'Where've you been?' Sandra narrowed her eyes suspiciously. 'You've been abroad haven't you? You can't fool yer old Auntie Sandra – I can tell from the tan. And you've thickened out a bit, too . . . in fact you look quite hunky. I could quite go for you . . .' She squeezed Leofred's bicep. 'Been somewhere nice? Turkey?'

'Israel, actually. It was . . . well, it was a sort of an experiment, I suppose. Only we decided – well, I decided, that we ought to come back before things went too far. So we . . . er, came back to England.'

'*We?*'

'Me, and my sister Heidi. She flew back with me today . . .'

Heidi had decided to blow fifteen pounds on a taxi. She couldn't face the tube.

Like Leofred, she took a detour via *Dick's*. Unlike Leofred, she was not surprised by the sign she found on the door. She asked the cab driver to take her back to her house in Knightsbridge.

The cleaning lady had been in to switch on the central heating, and the house was warm and welcoming. But there was no sign of Ivo, either there, or next door in his own house. Heidi was not sure whether she could face him or not, but she wanted to know where he was, and how he was.

She telephoned his office, but the imbecilic girl on the switchboard said he no longer worked in that building. She was obviously new, and didn't know what she was talking about. Heidi knew the type. She had probably just scraped out of school with O level flower-arranging. She insisted the girl put her through to Ivo's extension anyway, but the phone just rang and rang, with no-one answering.

Heidi lay back on her bed, closed her eyes and started to feel acutely depressed about leaving the kibbutz. Volunteers were only allowed to stay for six months at the most without a special permit, and Leofred had suggested that it would be easier to tear herself away sooner rather than later. He had been right, of course, but she was annoyed with him for being right. They had not spoken on the long bus journey from Kfar Hasava to Tel Aviv, or on the plane journey home.

Leofred had also had the nerve to say (or to hint, at least – Leofred could never actually come straight out with criticism) that life on the kibbutz was in some way making her lose her grip. He had been wrong about that, of course. She had been having a wonderful time. After Schaul, she had transferred to working in grapefruit and had spent a week sleeping with Gadi, one of Ilana's ex-lovers. Then she had had a fling with one of the soldiers home on a week's leave from his military service, a strapping young lad called . . . She racked her brain, but couldn't remember his name. Or his face. In fact, she couldn't really picture any of them now she was back.

For three whole days, Heidi more or less stayed where

she was – lying on her bed, feeling depressed. The phone, which had once hounded her to distraction, did not ring once.

On the fourth day, two things happened to make her snap out of her lethargy. First the phone rang, and it was Leofred. He sounded happy, but apologetic.

'I'm sorry,' he said. 'I've been thinking about it, and I realise I shouldn't have dragged you back with me. You could have had another four months there. I'm sorry.'

'Don't be,' Heidi replied, surprising herself. 'You did the right thing. Any longer and it would all have become a blur. It was a bit like a good party, and the secret with good parties is to leave while you're still having fun. I'm sorry I was such a crabby old cow. Am I forgiven?'

'Of course.'

'Good.'

Feeling better, Heidi decided to clear the pile of newspapers that was obstructing the doormat. As she picked them up, Ivo Cathcart stared up at her, his pig-like face looking rather cross.

In a state of shock she read the article which said he had sold up the entire Rapier Empire. It was a bit like learning that a relative had died. One that Heidi had resented, of course, but still admired. The article said that Mr Cathcart was giving no interviews, and that he planned to live quietly, away from the capital city.

Heidi had an idea.

She showered and changed and then ran outside and climbed into her Mercedes Sports. It had been a long time since she had driven anything other than a tractor, but after a certain amount of gear crashing she was on the road and heading out of London. She sang along to the radio, feeling happy now that she had found a sense of purpose again.

Cruising south towards Petersfield, a sign by the side of the road caught her eye. It looked somehow familiar. She slowed the car down to a crawl, and looked harder. It was the letters on the sign . . . she had definitely seen those handwritten capitals before . . .

'*SECOND HAND PORSCHES BOUGHT FOR CASH*'

Heidi glanced at the young man and the girl who were standing next to the sign. She stopped with a squealing of brakes.

'Jay! And Sas . . .'

But the girl at his side, stunning though she was, was not Saskia Cathcart.

'Sas. has split.' said Jay baldly. 'When the money ran out she didn't want to know.'

'Oh. I'm sorry.'

'But Joan here has been just brilliant. A real trooper . . .'

JOAN?!!

Heidi hadn't recognised her, and even if she had she would never have *dreamed* . . . She was flabbergasted by the change in the woman. And by the proprietorial way she was holding on to Jay's arm.

'So . . . how's business?' It was all she could think of to say.

'We're talking mega-potential,' said Jay, sounding exactly like the Jay of old. 'Mega-potential. We're on a real roll here. Loads of bankrupt whizz-kids are selling off their Porsches for nothing. I mean we're talking peanuts, pocket money. So we're going to smarten them up a bit and sell them off for a huge profit.'

'Can anyone still afford them?'

'Hey, life goes on, kid! We'll be flogging them to dentists and divorce lawyers—'

'And funeral directors,' chipped in Joan.

'Well, good luck . . . to both of you.'

Joan smiled broadly, and for the first time she looked truly pretty rather than just striking.

'Hey, how about you, Little Miss Mystery? What have you been up to? Check that tan! Are you—'

'Well, I'd better be pushing on.' Heidi was keen to avoid interrogation, and lengthly apologies for what had happened to the club.

'Going somewhere nice?' enquired Joan.

'I suppose you could say it's a voyage of discovery . . .'

Heidi could barely remember what the house looked like. But after all, she had only been there once before, two years ago.

She left the car at the bottom of the driveway, and as she strolled up towards the house, it all came back to her in a rush. She had been working on a documentary about Ivo Cathcart, entrepreneur extraordinary, and he had invited her down to a dinner party. His wife, Linda, had shot poisonous looks at Heidi all evening because she'd assumed Heidi was Ivo's mistress. And Heidi herself had expected Ivo to make a pass at her, but he hadn't. He'd wanted to, and she'd wanted him to, but he didn't, so she'd fallen in love with him. That was the way these things happened.

By the time Heidi reached the house, she was awash with nostalgia and the keen sense of expectancy that such reminiscences can incite. It was a cruel disappointment when no-one answered the door, not even after the third ring. She left the front porch and walked around the side of the house into the garden.

Ivo was on his hands and knees in a large swamp. (Heidi recollected that the swamp had once been a lawn, with a tennis court at its lower extremity.) He appeared to be trying to plant something, and was swearing a lot as he did so.

Heidi squelched up to him. 'Playing mud pies?' she enquired.

Ivo looked up, rubbing his hand across his forehead and forgetting that his hands were covered in soil. He rubbed his hands down his designer jeans and swore more loudly. Then he returned to his leeks, ignoring Heidi.

She had more or less expected this. 'Are those potatoes?' she asked, pointing to a pile of tubers.

'Yes – what of it?'

'It's the wrong time of year to plant them, that's all. You're several weeks too late for the late crop and about about six months too early for the early.'

A goat wandered into the swamp out of nowhere, trailing a rope from its collar, and began to eat the tops of the leeks. Ivo started to tussle with it. 'Well don't just stand there!' he snarled at Heidi, without looking at her.

Heidi picked her way over the goat, dragged it to the garden shed and tied its rope to the door handle. 'Is there anything else you'd like me to do?' she shouted to Ivo.

He flapped over to her in a pair of ill-fitting wellingtons borrowed from Crouch the gardener. His shirt sleeves were rolled up and Heidi noticed how muscular his forearms were.

'I'd rather you left now,' he said quietly. 'I don't think I can take any more of your coming and going. Not now. So unless you're an expert in animal husbandry, or agricultural methods, there's not a lot of point you being here.'

'Well I am actually,' said Heidi quickly. 'An expert, I mean. I've been working on a kibbutz in Israel, and I learned an awful lot.'

While Ivo watched, but pretended not to, Heidi milked the goat, and fed it, then fed the chickens and cleaned out the coop.

'You could put some manure on these leeks,' said Ivo

when she had finished. 'That is – if you're staying. I mean . . . really staying.'

Heidi rubbed her nose with a grubby finger as she considered this. She looked down at her suede court shoes, once red, now a shade of mud brown. Her Rifat Ozbek jacket was splattered with chicken shit.

' . . . Only things are different now, I want you to understand that. Life here is going to be very different to what we're used to. I'm Getting Back to Nature. I ripped the phone out yesterday, and I've put the TV out for the dustmen . . . and the video.'

'I'll think about it,' said Heidi finally. 'But in the meantime, why don't we take a look at those leeks? . . .'

Sammi-Dawn Thwort was in the sluice at the Everglade Nursing Home.

Taking advantage of a few minutes peace and privacy, she kicked off her ugly, low-heeled shoes and, since there were no chairs in the room, sat down on a dustbin.

It was still there, in the pocket of her green nylon overall. It made a crackling sound as she moved, the most satisfying sound in the whole world. She took it out and read it.

'*Dear Miss Thwort,*
It gives me great pleasure to confirm our acceptance of your mortgage application . . .'

Tonight Barry was taking her out to the Chinese to celebrate, but only after they had been to Decor-World to pick out their furniture. She'd already told Barry they were having pink and green all through – candy pink and peppermint green. And he'd said he'd let her choose the suite . . . she could hardly wait!

Grinning from ear to ear, Sammi-Dawn put away her letter and resumed her duties with the trolley. She wheeled it into the day-room and asked the old ladies if they fancied a cup of tea. She was still smiling broadly.

'Lovely girl,' observed Mrs Cartwright to Mrs Bentley. 'Nice and cheerful. Brightens the place up.'

'Like a Bourbon cream?' asked Sammi.

Mrs Bentley helped herself to three. 'Oh, yes,' she said to Mrs Cartwright. 'And such a pretty girl, too.'

The old ladies followed Sammi with their eyes as she wheeled the heavy trolley from the room.

'Very pretty.' agreed Mrs Cartwright. 'Blond hair, like that, a nice full figure . . . someone should tell her she could be a model . . .'

At the Bay Tree restaurant in Richmond, Leofred Plunkett was working very hard indeed.

There always seemed to be something that required his immediate attention, so that he rushed endlessly from one end of the restaurant to the other. The best way to describe it was 'bustling', although Leofred wasn't really that sort of person.

He had just taken delivery of the fresh flower arrangements and was about to climb up a stepladder and chalk up the wine prices when the chef called him from the kitchen. He squeezed his way back between the closely packed circular tables and through the double swing doors.

'Just wanted you to see this, Mr Plunkett.' said the chef, holding up a copper bottomed cauldron.

'Ah . . . what is it?'

'Sorrel soup. The lady boss said I was to get your approval when I wanted to put something new on the menu.'

'Very nice,' said Leofred, who wasn't quite sure what sorrel was, 'We'll include it.'

It was a bit of a joke, his being manager of a restaurant. But perhaps not as much of a joke as vice president of a multinational company, a post he had filled a mere three months earlier. At least this time he was enjoying himself.

''Ere, Leof, get yer backside in here!'

Sandra had arrived, and would be wanting the day's menus. He went into the dining room again to find her grinning all over her face.

'Have I got soup on my face?' he asked.

'No, no, nothing like that . . .' Sandra gave a deep sigh of contentment. 'I was just thinking how much I love this place!' She gazed fondly at the chintzy table cloths and the matching walls, hung with traditional prints. Julian was sitting at his desk in the corner, casting an eye over the accounts.

'Like his jumper?' Sandra asked. 'I just bought it for him, bless him.'

She took the menus that Leofred had prepared, and sat down at her typewriter to type them out. She had never lost the skills that made her queen of Drummond's typing pool, and her fingers were soon flying over the keyboard.

'What's this then?' Sandra squinted at the list. '*Squirrel soup?*'

'Sorrel. Sorrel soup.'

'I never could read your bleedin' handwriting, even when I was paid to.' Sandra grumbled. Then she looked up at Leofred and laughed. 'Does this remind you of anything?'

'Yes,' said Leofred. 'It's just like old times.'

Percy Grieves, brother of *Dick's* late handyman, was clearing out his garage.

He and his wife had just spent their life savings on a caravan, a nice little tourer, and he wanted to get the garage clean and swept before the dealer delivered it later that day. It wouldn't do to have their pride and joy standing in inches of filth and dust.

He was just getting the broom going around the edges of the concrete walls when he spotted something in the corner by the door. Something shiny. He went over and picked it up.

'A record . . .' he murmured to himself. Now how on earth had that got in there? It certainly didn't belong to him, or the missus . . .

Of course! It must have been in the van, and fallen or been dropped when the scrap merchant opened it up to take a look inside . . .

Percy was short-sighted, so he held the disc up close to his face in order to scrutinise its bright pink label.

'*Are . . . You . . . Feeling . . . Sexy?*.' he read, with difficulty. That was a bit saucy, wasn't it? and he'd never heard of this Sammi-Dawn Thwort bloke. Probably one of those darkies. Still, a record was a record, and it wasn't often you got something for nothing, was it? . . .

Feeling pleased with himself, Percy carried the record inside and placed it reverentially on the old manual operated turntable. And very soon, Sammi-Dawn Thwort's golden voice could be heard, floating over the roof-tops of suburban Kingston.

'*Touch my body; gimme a thrill*
I'm a wild beast and I'm ready to kill
Cos I'm feeling sexy, sexy as hell . . . '

EPILOGUE: Four months later

'... And now, on the Today programme, we have a special report on the post-crash sex revival. Sociologists are already dubbing it the Second Sexual Revolution, as formerly repressed and career-orientated yuppies seek to find themselves in a new flowering of sexual activity.

The drug at the centre of the controversy, freeing these Nouveaux Hippies from the fear of AIDS and pregnancy, is Contracon. Last month's figures showed record sales of this wonderdrug – claimed to have aphrodisiac side effects – as thousands of disillusioned young professionals flooded into high street chemists in search of a new sexual kick.

Strangest of all, when this product was first developed by Star Pharmaceuticals from a chemical called ZXT 45, commercial disaster was forecast. Now the company, bought four months ago from the Rapier Group by Ramberg Imperial ...'

Heidi Plunkett was listening closely to the radio; her one remaining link with the world of the media. She gazed through the drawing room window as she listened, chewing her lip.

Then she smiled. It was a beautiful spring morning, full of light and birdsong. Ivo, mucking out the pig-sty, was singing cheerfully to himself.

Heidi switched off the radio, picked up her hoe and went out to weed the vegetable patch.